ITALIAN-ENGLISH
ENGLISH-ITALIAN
DICTIONARY AND PHRASEBOOK

ITALIAN-ENGLISH
ENGLISH-ITALIAN
DICTIONARY AND PHRASEBOOK

Federica K. Clementi

HIPPOCRENE BOOKS
New York

Per Mia Madre e Mio Padre
To My Mother and Father

ISBN 0-7818-0812-X

For information, address:
HIPPOCRENE BOOKS, INC.
171 Madison Avenue
New York, NY 10016

Cataloging-in-Publication Data available from the
Library of Congress.

Printed in the United States of America.

CONTENTS

ABBREVIATIONS

adj.	adjective
adv.	adverb
amer.	American English
arch.	architectural
bot.	botanical
brit.	British English
coll.	colloquial
conj.	conjunction
etc.	et cetera
f.	feminine
interj.	interjection
m.	masculine
mec.	mechanical
mus.	musical
n.	noun
neol.	neologism
pl.	plural
prep.	preposition
pron.	pronoun
ref.	reflexive
s.	singular
v.	verb
v.int.	intransitive verb
v.t.	transitive verb

THE ITALIAN ALPHABET

Letter	*Italian name of the letter*
A	[a]
B	[bi]
C	[ci]
D	[di]
E	[e]
F	[effe]
G	[gi]
H	[acca]
I	[i]
L	[elle]
M	[emme]
N	[enne]
O	[o]
P	[pi]
Q	[qu]
R	[erre]
S	[esse]
T	[ti]
U	[u]
V	[vu]
Z	[zeta]

ITALIAN PRONUNCIATION

A	a: like a in far
B	b: like b in bar
C	c: like k in kite or c in cat, when followed by a, o, u
C	tch: like ch in China, when followed by e, i
Ch	c: like k in kite, always followed by e, i only
D	d: like d in door
E	è: like e in ten
E	é: like a in fate
F	f: like f in fire
G	g: like g in gap, when followed by a, o, u
G	dj: like j in jacket, job, when followed by e, i
Gh	g: like g in gap, always followed by e, i only
Gli	l (soft): similar to lli in billion
Gn	ñ: similar to ni in onion, like the Spanish ñ in niño
H	is always silent
I	ee: like i in machine
L	l: like l in letter
M	m: like m in mother
N	n: like n in nuts
O	o: like o in spot
P	p: like p in papaya
Q	q: like q in quick
R	r: strongly rolled
S	s: like s in simple
Sc	sk: like sk in skate, when followed by a, o, u
Sc	sh: like sh in shame, only when followed by i, e
T	t: like t in torn
U	oo: like oo in spoon
V	v: like v in victory
Z	z: like z in pizza
Z	ds: like ds in seeds

BASIC GRAMMAR

Word Order

There are no strict predetermined rules regarding how to construct a sentence in Italian. As a general rule, every sentence begins with the subject, followed by the verb and the complements.

In practice, the subject is omitted most of the time. In Italian the conjugation itself of the verb suggests who is the agent of the action. Therefore, the subject is understood from the person in which the verb is conjugated.

The negative sentence is constructed as follows:
Subject + negative particle (**non**) + verb + complements

A negative answer always starts with "no"; the negative particle before the verb is always "non":
(Io) non sono italiano. I am not Italian.
No, non sono italiano. No, I am not Italian.

Genders, singular and plural
(I generi, singolare e plurale)

In Italian, nouns are either masculine or feminine in gender and singular or plural in number.

child
bambino (masculine, singular)
bambini (masculine, plural)
bambina (feminine, singular)
bambine (feminine, plural)

friend
amico (masculine, singular)
amici (masculine, plural)
amica (feminine, singular)
amiche (feminine, plural)

professor
professore (masculine, singular)
professori (masculine, plural)
professoressa (feminine, singular)
professoresse (feminine, plural)

table
tavolo (masculine, singular)
tavoli (masculine, plural)

chair
sedia (feminine, singular)
sedie (feminine, plural)

exercise book
quaderno (masculine, singular)
quaderni (masculine, plural)

pen
penna (feminine, singular)
penne (feminine, plural)

The Article (L'articolo)

The Italian definite articles are:

Singular
il - masculine singular, for example: **il bambino, il padre**.
lo - masculine singular form for all words starting with
a vowel, s + consonant, z: for example: **l'albero,
lo straniero, lo zio**.
la - feminine singular, for example: **la madre, la zia**.

Plural
i - masculine plural, for example: **i bambini, i padri**.
gli - masculine plural for all words starting with a
vowel, s + consonant, z, for example: **gli alberi, gli
stranieri, gli zii**.
le - feminine plural, for example: **le madri, le zie**.

The indefinite articles are:

un - masculine, for example: **un bambino, un tavolo**.
uno - masculine for all words starting with s +
consonant, z, for example: **uno straniero, uno zio**.
una - feminine, for example: **una madre, una zia**. If
the word starts with a vowel, **una** becomes **un'**, for
example: **un'amica**.

The Adjective (L'aggettivo)

Italian adjectives agree in gender and number with the
noun they refer to:

buono - (good)
buon - masculine singular, for example: **un buon giorno**.
buono - masculine singular form of all words starting
with a vowel, s + consonant, z, for example: **un
buono sconto**.
buona - feminine singular, for example: **una buona
madre**.
buoni - masculine plural, for example: **buoni amici**.
buone - feminine plural, for example: **buone amiche**.

Attention: Italian adjectives ending in **-e** remain unchanged
in the masculine singular and feminine singular, while
taking an **-i** in both masculine and feminine plural:

grande - (big, large)
il **grande** palazzo (masculine singular)
i **grandi** palazzi (masculine plural)
la **grande** famiglia (feminine singular)
le **grandi** famiglie (feminine plural)

Personal pronouns (Pronomi personali)

I **io**
you **tu**
he **egli**

she **ella**
we **noi**
you **voi**
they m. **essi**
they f. **esse**

The verb (Il verbo)

Present (Presente)

The Italian verb in the present tense has three conjugations, recognizable by the infinitive verb ending.

1) First conjugation: verbs ending in **-are**
2) Second conjugation: verbs ending in **-ere**
3) Third conjugation: verbs ending in **-ire**

1) PARLARE, VISITARE, GIOCARE, GUARDARE, VOLARE, FUMARE, CUCINARE, etc.:

io parl**o**
tu parl**i**
egli/ella parl**a**
noi parl**iamo**
voi parl**ate**
essi/esse parl**ano**

2) VEDERE, SCRIVERE, CREDERE, PIANGERE, etc.:

io ved**o**
tu ved**i**
egli/ella ved**e**
noi ved**iamo**
voi ved**ete**
essi/esse ved**ono**

3) SENTIRE, PARTIRE, OFFRIRE, etc.:

io sent**o**
tu sent**i**

egli/ella sent**e**
noi sent**iamo**
voi sent**ite**
essi/esse sent**ono**

Modal verbs (Verbi modali)

CAN **POTERE**
io **posso**
tu **puoi**
egli/ella **può**
noi **possiamo**
voi **potete**
essi/esse **possono**

WILL **VOLERE**
io **voglio**
tu **vuoi**
egli/ella **vuole**
noi **vogliamo**
voi **volete**
essi/esse **vogliono**

MUST **DOVERE**
io **devo**
tu **devi**
egli/ella **deve**
noi **dobbiamo**
voi **dovete**
essi/esse **devono**

Simple Past (Passato Remoto)

TO BE **ESSERE**
io fui I was
tu fosti you were

egli/ella fu he/she was
noi fummo we were
voi foste you were
essi/esse furono they were

TO HAVE **AVERE**
io ebbi I had
tu avesti you had
egli/ella ebbe he/she had
noi avemmo we had
voi aveste you had
essi/esse ebbero they had

The simple past of the model verbs is formed as follows:

TO SPEAK **PARLARE**
io parlai I spoke
tu parlasti you spoke
egli/ella parlò he/she spoke
noi parlammo we spoke
voi parlaste you spoke
essi/esse parlarono they spoke

TO GO **ANDARE**
io andai I went
tu andasti you went
egli/ella andò he/she went
noi andammo we went
voi andaste you went
essi/esse andarono they went

TO SELL **VENDERE**
io vendei I sold
tu vendesti you sold
egli/ella vendè he/she sold
noi vendemmo we sold
voi vendeste you sold
essi/esse vendettero they sold

TO SIT **SEDERE**
io sedei I sat
tu sedesti you sat
egli/ella sedette he/she sat
noi sedemmo we sat
voi sedeste you sat
essi/esse sedettero they sat

TO HEAR **SENTIRE**
io sentii I heard
tu sentisti you heard
egli/ella sentì he/she heard
noi sentimmo we heard
voi sentiste you heard
essi/esse sentirono they heard

TO LEAVE **PARTIRE**
io partii I left
tu partisti you left
egli/ella partì he/she left
noi partimmo we left
voi partiste you left
essi/esse partirono they left

Many Italian verbs are irregular in the simple past tense. Here are only some of them and their respective conjugations:

TO ANSWER **RISPONDERE**
io risposi I answered
tu rispondesti you answered
egli/ella rispose he/she answered
noi rispondemmo we answered
voi rispondeste you answered
essi/esse risposero they answered

TO MAKE **FARE**
io feci I made
tu facesti you made
egli/ella fece he/she made

noi facemmo we made
voi faceste you made
essi/esse fecero they made

TO ASK **CHIEDERE**
io chiesi I asked
tu chiedesti you asked
egli/ella chiese he/she asked
noi chiedemmo we asked
voi chiedeste you asked
essi/esse chiesero they asked

TO COME **VENIRE**
io venni I came
tu venisti you came
egli/ella venne he/she came
noi venimmo we came
voi veniste you came
essi/esse vennero they came

Note:
There is a general pattern in the irregularity of such irregular verbs.
(a) Second person singular, first person plural, second person plural are always regular.
(b) The remaining three irregular forms, corresponding to the first and third person singular and third person plural, always have the same irregular root. Therefore, it is sufficient to know the first person singular of an irregular verb in the simple past, then simply change the ending **-i** into **-e** to obtain the third person singular or into **-ero** to obtain the third person plural. For example: **piangere** (to cry) in the simple past is **io piansi**, **egli pianse**, **essi piansero**, etc.

Present Perfect (Passato Prossimo)

The present perfect in Italian is formed by the present of the auxiliary verb "to have" or "to be," followed by the past participle form of the verb. The auxiliary "to be" is used only with those verbs indicating or implying motion and movement from one place to another, a state or a change of state, or a mood.

Examples:

scrivere - infinitive - (to write)
scritto - past participle
io ho scritto - present perfect - (I have written, I wrote)

venire - infinitive - (to come)
venuto - past participle
io sono venuto - present perfect - (I have come, I came)

When a verb is conjugated with **essere** (to be) the past participle agrees with the subject in gender and number.

Examples:

Il ragazzo ha scritto una lettera. The boy has written a letter.
I ragazzi hanno scritto una lettera. The boys have written a letter.

La ragazza ha scritto una lettera. The girl has written a letter.
Le ragazze hanno scritto una lettera. The girls have written a letter.

But:

Il ragazzo è venuto ieri. The boy came yesterday.
I ragazzi sono venuti ieri. The boys came yesterday.

La ragazza è venuta ieri. The girl came yesterday.
Le ragazze sono venute ieri. The girls came yesterday.

Imperfect (Imperfetto)

The imperfect tense refers to an action that took place in the past, for a certain period of time—with the focus on the duration of the action/event expressed by the verb— or to an action that used to happen in the past, but is now completed.

TO BE **ESSERE**
io ero I used to be; I was
tu eri you used to be; you were
egli/ella era he/she used to be; he/she was
noi eravamo we used to be; we were
voi eravate you used to be; you were
essi/esse erano they used to be; they were

TO HAVE **AVERE**
io avevo I used to have; I had
tu avevi you used to have; you had
egli/ella aveva he/she used to have; he/she had
noi avevamo we used to have; we had
voi avevate you used to have; you had
essi/esse avevano they used to have; they had

The endings of the three conjugations in the imperfect tense are identical:

TO SPEAK **PARLARE**
io parlavo I used to speak; I spoke
tu parlavi you used to speak; you spoke
egli/ella parlava he/she used to speak; he/she spoke
noi parlavamo we used to speak; we spoke
voi parlavate you used to speak; you spoke
essi/esse parlavano they used to speak; they spoke

TO MAKE **FARE**
io facevo I used to make; I made
tu facevi you used to make; you made

egli/ella faceva he/she used to make; he/she made
noi facevamo we used to make; we made
voi facevate you used to make; you made
essi/esse facevano they used to make; they made

TO SEE **VEDERE**
io vedevo I used to see; I saw
tu vedevi you used to see; you saw
egli/ella vedeva he/she used to see; he/she saw
noi vedevamo we used to see; we saw
voi vedevate you used to see; you saw
essi/esse vedevano they used to see; they saw

TO DRINK **BERE**
io bevevo I used to drink; I drank
tu bevevi you used to drink; you drank
egli/ella beveva he/she used to drink; he/she drank
noi bevevamo we used to drink; we drank
voi bevevate you used to drink; you drank
essi/esse bevevano they used to drink; they drank

TO LEAVE **PARTIRE**
io partivo I used to leave; I left
tu partivi you used to leave; you left
egli/ella partiva he/she used to leave; he/she left
noi partivamo we used to leave; we left
voi partivate you used to leave; you left
essi/esse partivano they used to leave; they left

TO SAY **DIRE**
io dicevo I used to say; I said
tu dicevi you used to say; you said
egli/ella diceva he/she used to say; he/she said
noi dicevamo we used to say; we said
voi dicevate you used to say; you said
essi/esse dicevano they used to say; they said

Note:
(To use the verb 'to do' as an example:) "I was doing, you were doing, he/she was doing, we were doing, you were doing, they were doing" is also an acceptable English translation.

The Future (Il Futuro)

The endings of the verbs in the future tense for all of the conjugations are:

1st sing. **-ò**
2nd sing. **-ai**
3rd sing. **-à**
1st pl. **-emo**
2nd pl. **-ete**
3rd pl. **-anno**

PARLARE
io parlerò I will talk
tu parlerai you will talk
egli/ella parlerà he/she will talk
noi parleremo we will talk
voi parlerete you will talk
essi/esse parleranno they will talk

VENDERE
io venderò (I will sell)
tu venderai
egli/ella venderà
noi venderemo
voi venderete
essi/esse venderanno

SENTIRE
io sentirò (I will hear)
tu sentirai
egli/ella sentirà
noi sentiremo
voi sentirete
essi/esse sentiranno

POTERE
io potrò (I will be able)
tu potrai
egli/ella potrà

noi potremo
voi potrete
essi/esse potranno

Note:
In the future tense, for verbs of the first conjugation the
-a of the ending (**-are**) becomes **-e** or is sometimes
dropped.

The verb "to be" in the future tense is declined as follows:

ESSERE
io sarò
tu sarai
egli/ella sarà
noi saremo
voi sarete
essi/esse saranno

A number of verbs drop the vowel between the root and
the ending, for example:

andare - **io andrò**
potere - **io potrò**
vivere - **io vivrò**

The conditional mood (Il condizionale)

The conditional is formed by keeping the same stem as the
future tense and adding the following endings:

1st sing. **-ei**
2nd sing. **-esti**
3rd sing. **-ebbe**
1st pl. **-emmo**
2nd pl. **-este**
3rd pl. **-ebbero**

Therefore, all changes in the root occurring in the future
tense will also occur in the conditional.

TO EAT **MANGIARE**
io mangerei I would eat
tu mangeresti you would eat
egli/ella mangerebbe he/she would eat
noi mangeremmo we would eat
voi mangereste you would eat
essi/esse mangerebbero they would eat

POTERE
io potrei (I could)
tu potresti
egli/ella potrebbe
noi potremmo
voi potreste
essi/esse potrebbero

VENIRE
io verrei (I would come)
tu verresti
egli/ella verrebbe
noi verremmo
voi verreste
essi/esse verrebbero

ESSERE
io sarei (I would be)
tu saresti
egli/ella sarebbe
noi saremmo
voi sareste
essi/esse sarebbero

Reflexive verbs (Il riflessivo)

The reflexive verbs imply an action done or directed to oneself, or an action which implies reciprocity between two or more subjects. In Italian, the infinitive of the reflexive verbs can be identified by the pronoun **-si** which is added to the regular ending of the infinitive (from which the **-e** is dropped): **-arsi**, **-ersi**, **-irsi** are the endings of the reflexive verb.

TO GET UP **ALZARSI**

io mi alzo I get (myself) up
tu ti alzi you get (yourself) up
egli/ella si alza he/she gets (him/herself) up
noi ci alziamo we get (ourselves) up
voi vi alzate you get (yourselves) up
essi/esse si alzano they get (themselves) up

TO WASH ONESELF **LAVARSI**

io mi lavo
tu ti lavi
egli/ella si lava
noi ci laviamo
voi vi lavate
essi/esse si lavano

Some of the main irregular verbs in Italian:

Presente	**Passato Remoto**	**Participio Passato**	
accendere	accesi	acceso	to turn on
aprire	aprii (apersi)	aperto	to open
assumere	assunsi	assunto	to assume
bere	bevvi	bevuto	to drink
cadere	caddi	caduto	to fall
chiedere	chiesi	chiesto	to ask
conoscere	conobbi	conosciuto	to meet
correre	corsi	corso	to run
crescere	crebbi	cresciuto	to grow
cuocere	cossi	cotto	to cook
dare	diedi	dato	to give
dire	dissi	detto	to say
discutere	discussi	discusso	to discuss
dividere	divisi	diviso	to divide
dovere	dovetti	dovuto	must
esistere	esistei	esistito	to exist
esplodere	esplosi	esploso	to explode

essere	fui	stato	to be
fare	feci	fatto	to do
invadere	invasi	invaso	to invade
leggere	lessi	letto	to read
mettere	misi	messo	to put
mordere	morsi	morso	to bite
muovere	mossi	mosso	to move
nascere	nacqui	nato	to be born
nascondere	nascosi	nascosto	to hide
offendere	offesi	offeso	to offend
offrire	offersi (offrii)	offerto	to offer
perdere	persi	perso	to lose
piacere	piacqui	piaciuto	to please, like
piangere	piansi	pianto	to cry
piovere	piovve	piovuto	to rain
potere	potei	potuto	can
prendere	presi	preso	to take
proteggere	protessi	protetto	to protect
reggere	ressi	retto	to hold
ridere	risi	riso	to laugh
rimanere	rimasi	rimasto	to stay
rispondere	risposi	risposto	to answer
rompere	ruppi	rotto	to break
salire	salii	salito	to get on
sapere	seppi	saputo	to know
scegliere	scelsi	scelto	to choose
scendere	scesi	sceso	to go down
scrivere	scrissi	scritto	to write
sedere	sedetti	seduto	to sit
spegnere	spensi	spento	to switch off
spendere	spesi	speso	to spend
stare	stetti	stato	to stay
tacere	tacqui	taciuto	to be quiet
tenere	tenni	tenuto	to keep
trarre	trassi	tratto	to take out
uccidere	uccisi	ucciso	to kill
vedere	vidi	veduto/visto	to see
venire	venni	venuto	to come

vincere	vinsi	vinto	to win
volere	volli	voluto	to want

The comparative (Il comparativo)

Italian has three comparative forms: *comparativo di uguaglianza*, *comparativo di maggioranza*, and *comparativo di minoranza*.

Comparativo di uguaglianza, "… come," "tanto quanto", corresponds to the comparative English form "as (much) … as," "so (much) … as."

Comparativo di maggioranza "più … di" corresponds to the English form "more … than."

Comparativo di minoranza "meno … di" corresponds to the English form "less … than."

Examples:

Paolo è **più alto di** Maria. Paul is **taller than** Mary.

Maria è **più bassa di** Paolo. Mary is **shorter than** Paul.

New York è **più grande di** Boston. New York is **bigger than** Boston.

Boston è **più piccola di** New York. Boston is **smaller than** New York.

Il vino rosso è **più dolce del** vino bianco. Red wine is **sweeter than** white wine.

La Grecia è **meno cara dell'**Italia. Greece is **less expensive than** Italy.

Giovanni è **meno ricco di** Marco. John is **less rich than** Mark.

Sono **tanto felice quanto** te. I am **as happy as** you are.

Puoi mangiare **tanto quanto** vuoi. You can eat **as much as** you want.

Costa **tanto quanto** vale. It costs **as much as** it is worth.

Note: When the terms of the comparison are both adjectives, nouns, adverbs, indirect complements or verbs, the form **più … che** is used instead of **più … di**.

Examples:

La mia macchina è **più comoda che** bella. My car is **more comfortable than** beautiful.

Mangio **più frutta che** verdura. I eat **more fruits than** vegetables.

A mio figlio **piace più** leggere un libro **che** giocare. My son **likes better** reading a book **than** playing.

Decido **più istintivamente che** razionalmente. I decide **more instinctively than** rationally.

Relative superlative (Superlativo relativo)

The Italian superlativo relativo corresponds to the English "the most... (of)," "the least... (of)."

It is composed as follows: article + **più** + adjective + **di**

Examples:

Marcello è **il ragazzo più alto**. Marcello is the tallest boy.

Marcello è **il più alto della** sua classe. Marcello is **the tallest of** his class.

Roma è **la città più cara** d'Italia. Rome is **the most expensive town** in Italy.

Questo è stato **il più bel** viaggio **della** mia vita. This was **the most beautiful** trip **of** my life.

Absolute superlative (Superlativo assoluto)

The absolute superlative is formed by adding the suffix **-issimo** to the adjective, or using **molto**, **tanto**, **assai**, **ultra**, **arci**, or **super** before the adjective.

Examples:

È un film **bellissimo**. It's a **marvelous** movie.

È un ristorante **elegantissimo**. It's a **very elegant** restaurant.

Quel negozio è **super caro**. That store is **very expensive**.

Irregular comparative and superlative forms (Comparativi e superlativi irregolari)

good (adjective): buono - migliore - ottimo
good (adverb): bene - meglio - benissimo
bad (adjective): cattivo - peggiore - pessimo
bad (adverb): male - peggio - malissimo (pessimamente)
much (adverb): molto - più - moltissimo
less (adverb): poco - meno - pochissimo

Examples:

Ho mangiato la pizza **peggiore** del mondo! I ate the **worst** pizza in the world!

A Parigi ho bevuto il **migliore** vino del mondo! I drank the **best** wine in the world in Paris!

È il libro **meno interessante** di tutti. It's the **least interesting** book of all.

Possessive (Il possessivo)

mio	my
tuo	your
suo	his
nostro	our
vostro	your
loro	their

The possessive adjectives agree in gender and number with the word to which they refer. The possessive adjectives are always preceded by the article, except when they refer to family members and only when these are in the singular. The article is then omitted.

Examples:

Questa è **la mia** casa. This is my home.
Ecco **le tue** chiavi. Here are your keys.
La vostra amica è molto gentile. Your girlfriend is
   very kind.
Mio padre ha 60 anni. My father is 60 years old.
Mia cugina ha un bellissimo gatto. My cousin has a
   beautiful cat.
Mio fratello è più alto di me. My brother is taller than I.
I miei fratelli sono tutti più alti di me. All my brothers
   are taller than I.
Le mie due cugine sono sorelle gemelle. My two
   cousins are twin sisters.

Therefore, the possessive adjective is declined as follows:

masculine singular
(il) mio
(il) tuo
(il) suo
(il) nostro
(il) vostro
(il) loro

masculine plural
(i) miei
(i) tuoi
(i) suoi
(i) nostri
(i) vostri
(i) loro

feminine singular
(la) mia
(la) tua
(la) sua
(la) nostra

(la) vostra
(la) loro

feminine plural
(le) mie
(le) tue
(le) sue
(le) nostre
(le) vostre
(le) loro

Whose... is this...? (Di chi è...?)
Di chi è questo passaporto? **Whose** passport is this?
È mio. It's mine.
È il mio passaporto. It's my passport.
Mio! Mine!

Questions

Questions are formed through means of intonation. Only the intonation, that is the stress put on certain words or parts of the sentence, will indicate the difference between an affirmative sentence and a question.

Interrogative pronouns (Pronomi interrogativi)

come	how
quando	when
dove	where
chi	who, whom
di chi	whose
quale	which, what
che, che cosa	what
perché	why, because
quanto	how much
quanti	how many

ITALIAN-ENGLISH DICTIONARY

A

a *prep.* at, in
abbaiare *v.* to bark
abbastanza *adv.* enough
abbazia *n.f.* abbey
abbisognare *v.* to need
abbondante *adj.* plentiful
abbondanza *n.f.* abundance
abbracciare *v.* to embrace
abbraccio *n.m.* embrace
abbreviazione *n.f.* abbreviation
abbronzatura *n.f.* tan
abile *adj.* capable, able, skillful
abitazione *n.f.* house, dwelling place
abitudine *n.f.* habit
aborrire *v.* to abhor
abusare *v.* to abuse
accadere *v.* to happen
accappatoio *n.m.* bath robe
accendere *v.* to switch
accensione *n.f.* ignition
accessorio *n.m.* accessories *pl.*
accettare *v.* to accept
accettazione *n.f.* check-in
acciaio *n.m.* steel
acciuga *n.f.* anchovy
accoltellare *v.* to stab
acconto *n.m.* account
accorciare *v.* to shorten
accordarsi *v.ref.* to agree
accordo *n.m.* agreement
accusa *n.f.* accusation
accusare *v.* to accuse
aceto *n.m.* vinegar

acqua *n.f.* water
acquisto *n.m.* purchase, shopping
aculeo *n.m.* sting
acuto *adj.* smart, acute
adatto *adj.* fit
Addio! *interj.* Good-bye!
addome *n.m.* abdomen
adulare *v.* to flatter
adulatore *n.m.* flatterer
adulto *n.m., adj.* adult
aereo *n.m.* airplane
aeroplano *n.m.* airplane
aeroporto *n.m.* airport
affamato *adj.* hungry
affare *n.m.* business
affilare *v.* to sharpen
affilato *adj.* sharp
affittare *v.* to rent
affitto *n.m.* rent
affrettarsi *v.* to hurry
Africa *n.f.* Africa
aggiornato *adj.* up-to-date
aggiungere *v.* to add
agitazione *n.f.* agitation, anxiety
aglio *n.m.* garlic
agnello *n.m.* lamb
ago *n.m.* needle
agosto *n.m.* August
aiutare *v.* to help
aiuto *n.m.* help
ala *n.f.* wing
alabastro *n.m.* alabaster
alba *n.f.* daybreak
albero *n.m.* tree
albicocca *n.f.* apricot
alcol *n.m.* alcohol
alfabeto *n.m.* alphabet
allacciare *v.* to tie
allergia *n.f.* allergy

allergico *adj.* allergic
alloggio *n.m.* accommodation
almanacco *n.m.* calendar
almeno *adv.* at least
altezza *n.f.* height
alto *adj.* high, tall
altrimenti *adv.* otherwise
altro *adj., pron.* another, other
altrove *adv.* elsewhere
amante *n.m., n.f.* lover
amare *v.* to love
amaro *adj.* bitter
ambizione *n.f.* ambitious
ambulanza *n.f.* ambulance
America *n.f.* America
americano *n.m., adj.* American
amichevole *adj.* friendly
amico *n.m.* friend
amido *n.m.* starch
ammalato *n.m., adj.* ill, sick
ammirare *v.* to admire
ammissione *n.f.* admission
amore *n.m.* love
ampio *adj.* broad, large
analcolico *adj.* non-alcoholic
ananas *n.m.* pineapple
anatra *n.f.* duck
anche *adv.* also
ancora *adv.* again, yet
àncora *n.f.* anchor
andare *v.* to go
anello *n.m.* ring
anestetico *n.m., adj.* anesthetic
angelo *n.m.* angel
angolo *n.m.* corner
anima *n.f.* soul
animale *n.m.* animal
anniversario *n.m.* anniversary
anno *n.m.* year

annunciare *v.* to announce
anteriore *adj.* front; former, previous
antibiotico *n.m.* antibiotic
antidepressivo *n.m.* antidepressant
antidolorifico *adj.* painkiller
antipasto *n.m.* appetizer
antiquariato *n.m.* antiques *pl.*
antiquario *n.m.* antique shop
antisettico *n.m.* antiseptic
ape *n.f.* bee
aperitivo *n.m.* aperitif
aperto *adj.* open
appartamento *n.m.* apartment
appena *adv.* barely, just (only)
appendere *v.* to hang
appendicite *n.f.* appendicitis
appetito *n.m.* hunger, appetite
appuntamento *n.m.* appointment
apribottiglie *n.f.* bottle opener
aprile *n.m.* April
aprire *v.* to open
aquila *n.f.* eagle
aragosta *n.f.* lobster
arancia *n.f.* orange
archeologia *n.f.* archaeology
architetto *n.m.* architect
arcobaleno *n.m.* rainbow
argento *n.m.* silver
aria *n.f.* air
arido *adj.* arid
aringa *n.f.* herring
arma *n.m.* weapon
armadio *n.m.* closet, wardrobe
aroma *n.m.* flavor, aroma, zest
arrabbiarsi *v.ref.* to be or to get angry
arrabbiato *adj.* angry, cross
arrestare *v.* to arrest
arrivare *v.* to arrive

arrivo *n.m.* arrival
arte *n.f.* art
arteria *n.f.* artery
artificiale *adj.* artificial
artista *n.m.* artist
ascensore *n.m.* elevator (amer.), lift (brit.)
asciugacapelli *n.m.* hair dryer
asciugamano *n.m.* towel
asciugare *v.* to dry
asciutto *adj.* dry, dried
ascoltare *v.* to listen
Asia *n.f.* Asia
asino *n.m.* donkey
asma *n.m.* asthma
asparago *n.m.* asparagus
aspettare *v.* to wait
aspirapolvere *n.m.* vacuum cleaner
aspirina *n.f.* aspirin
aspro *adj.* sour, bitter
assaggiare *v.* to taste
assassinio *n.m.* murder
assassino *n.m.* murderer, killer
assegno *n.m.* check
assente *adj.* absent
assetato *adj.* thirsty
assicurare *v.* to assure
assicurazione *n.f.* insurance
assolato *adj.* sunny
assortimento *n.m.* assortment
assumere *v.* to hire
assurdità *n.f.* nonsense, absurdity
assurdo *adj.* absurd
attaccapanni *n.m.* hanger (clothes)
attacco *n.m.* attack
attento *adj.* careful
attenzione *n.f.* care, attention
Attenzione! *interj.* Beware!
attitudine *n.f.* skill, ability, aptitude; attitude
attività *n.f.* activity, business

atto *n.m.* act
attore *n.m.* actor
attraente *adj.* attractive
attraversare *v.* to cross
attraverso *adv., prep.* through
attrice *n.f.* actress
augurare *v.* to wish
auguri *(pl.) n.m.* congratulations
augurio *n.m.* wish
Austria *n.f.* Austria
autobus *n.m.* bus
automatico *adj.* automatic
autostima *n.f.* self-esteem
autostoppista *(neol.) n.m.* hitchhiker
autunno *n.m.* autumn, fall
avanti *adv.* forward
avanzi *(pl.) n.m.* remainder, remains, leftovers
avere *v.* to have
avorio *n.m.* ivory
avvelenato *adj.* poisoning
avventura *n.f.* adventure
avviso *n.m.* notice
avvocato *n.m.* lawyer, advocate
azione *n.f.* action
azzurro *adj.* blue

B

baciare *v.* to kiss
bacio *n.m.* kiss
baffi *(pl.) n.m.* moustache *s.*
bagaglio *n.m.* baggage, luggage
bagnato *adj.* wet
bagno *n.m.* bath
baia *n.f.* bay
balconata *n.f.* balcony, gallery
balcone *n.m.* balcony
balena *n.f.* whale

ballare *v.* to dance
balletto *n.m.* ballet
bambinaia *n.f.* babysitter
bambola *n.f.* doll
banana *n.f.* banana
banca *n.f.* bank
bandiera *n.f.* flag
bar *n.m.* café
barba *n.f.* beard
barbiere *n.m.* barber
barca *n.f.* boat
barella *n.f.* stretcher
barile *n.m.* barrel
Barocco *n.m.* Baroque
basilica *n.f.* basilica
basilico *n.m.* basil
basso *adj., adv.* low, short, small
basta! *interj.* enough!
battaglia *n.f.* battle
batteria *n.f.* battery
battesimo *n.m.* baptism
beffarsi *v.* to fool, to mock
bellezza *n.f.* beauty
bello *adj.* beautiful, handsome
benedire *v.* to bless
benvenuto *n.m.* welcome
benzina *n.f.* gasoline
bere *v.* to drink
bianco *adj.* white
bibita *n.f.* drink
biblioteca *n.f.* library
bicchiere *n.m.* glass
bicicletta *n.f.* bicycle
biglietto *n.m.* card, ticket, pass
bilancia *n.f.* scale
bimbo *n.m.* baby
biografia *n.f.* biography
birra *n.f.* beer
biscotto *n.m.* biscuit

bisogno *n.m.* need
bistecca *n.f.* steak
bloccare *v.* to block
bocca *n.f.* mouth
bolla *n.f.* blister
bollente *adj.* hot
bollire *v.* to boil
bollitore *n.m.* kettle
borsa *n.f.* bag
borsetta *n.f.* handbag, purse
botanica *n.f.* botany
bottiglia *n.f.* bottle
bracciale *n.m.* bracelet
braccio *n.m.* arm
bramare *v.* to yearn, to long for
breve *adj.* brief, short
brillare *v.* to shine
brina *n.f.* frost
bronzo *n.m.* bronze
bruciare *v.* to burn
brutto *adj.* ugly
buco *n.m.* hole
bugiardo *n.m.* liar
buio *adj.* dark
buono *adj.* good
burro *n.m.* butter
bussare *v.* to knock
bussola *n.f.* compass
busta *n.f.* envelope

C

cabina *n.f.* cabin, booth
cacciatore *n.m.* hunter
cadere *v.* to fall
caduta *n.f.* fall, drop
caffè *n.m.* coffee
caffeina *n.f.* caffeine

caldo *adj.* warm
calendario *n.m.* calendar
calma *n.f.* calm
calore *n.m.* heat, warmth
calza *n.f.* stocking
calzettoni *(pl.) n.m.* socks
cambiare *v.* to change, to exchange
cambio *n.m.* currency, exchange rate; gear (mec.)
cameriera *n.f.* waitress
cameriere *n.m.* waiter
camicia *n.f.* blouse, shirt
camminare *v.* to walk
campagna *n.f.* countryside
campanello *n.m.* bell
campeggiare *v.* to camp, to go camping
campo *n.m.* field
cancello *n.m.* gate
cancro *n.m.* cancer
candela *n.f.* candle
cane *n.m.* dog
cannella *n.f.* cinnamon
cantante *n.m.* singer
cantare *v.* to sing
cantiere *n.m.* yard, shipyard, building yard
canzone *n.f.* song
capelli *(pl.) n.m.* hair *s.*
capire *v.* to understand
capitale *n.f.* capital
capitello *n.m.* capital (arch.)
capo *n.m.* head, chief, leader, boss
capodanno *n.m.* New Year's Eve
capolinea *n.m.* bus stop
cappella *n.f.* chapel
cappello *n.m.* hat
cappero *n.m.* caper
cappotto *n.m.* coat
capra *n.f.* goat
carburante *n.m.* fuel

carciofo *n.m.* artichoke
carenza *n.f.* shortage, lack
carino *adj.* nice, neat
carne *n.f.* meat
caro *adj.* dear, expensive
carota *n.f.* carrot
carpa *n.f.* carp
carta *n.f.* paper
cartello *n.m.* sign-board, sign
cartina *n.f.* map
cartolina *n.f.* postcard
casa *n.f.* home
casalinga *n.f.* housewife
cascata *n.f.* waterfall
cassa *n.f.* cashier
casseruola *n.f.* saucepan
cassetto *n.m.* drawer
castagna *n.f.* chestnut
castello *n.m.* castle
catacomba *n.f.* catacomb
catalogo *n.m.* catalog
catena *n.f.* chain
cattedrale *n.f.* cathedral
cattivo *adj.* bad
cattolico *adj.* catholic
cautela *n.f.* caution
cavallo *n.m.* horse
cavatappi *n.m.* corkscrew
caviglia *n.f.* ankle
cavolfiore *n.m.* cauliflower
cavolo *n.m.* cabbage
ceci *(pl.) n.m.* chickpeas
cena *n.f.* dinner, supper
cenare *v.* to dine, to have dinner
centimetro *n.m.* centimeter
centinaia *(pl.) n.f.* hundreds
centro *n.m.* center
ceramica *n.f.* ceramic
cerniera *n.f.* zipper

cerotto *n.m.* band-aid
certificato *n.m.* certificate
certo *adj.* of course, sure
cervello *n.m.* brain
cetriolo *n.m.* cucumber
che *pron.* what, that
chi *pron.* who
chiamare *v.* to call
chiaro *adj.* clear
chiave *n.f.* key
chicco *n.m.* grain
chiedere *v.* to ask for
chiesa *n.f.* church
chilogrammo *n.m.* kilogram
chilometro *n.m.* kilometer
chiodo *n.m.* nail
chiosco *n.m.* kiosk
chirurgia *n.f.* surgery
chirurgo *n.m.* surgeon
chitarra *n.f.* guitar
chiudere *v.* to close
chiunque *pron.* anyone, anybody
chiuso *adj.* closed
Ciao! *interj.* Hi!
cibo *n.m.* food
cicogna *n.f.* stork
cicoria *n.f.* chicory
cielo *n.m.* sky
ciglia *(pl.) n.m.* eyelashes
ciliegia *n.f.* cherry
cimitero *n.m.* cemetery
cinema *n.m.* cinema
cinese *adj.* Chinese
cinta *n.f.* belt
cioccolata *n.f.* chocolate
cipolla *n.f.* onion
circa *adv.* about
circolo *n.m.* circle
citare *v.* to quote

citazione *n.f.* quotation
città *n.f.* city, town
cittadino *n.m.* citizen
classe *n.f.* class
cliente *n.m.* customer, client
clima *n.m.* climate
cognata *n.f.* sister-in-law
cognato *n.m.* brother-in-law
cognome *n.m.* surname, family name
colazione *n.f.* breakfast
colla *n.f.* glue
collana *n.f.* necklace
collina *n.f.* hill
collo *n.m.* neck
colore *n.m.* color
colpa *n.f.* fault, guilt
colpire *v.* to hit
coltello *n.m.* knife
come *adv.* as, how
commedia *n.f.* comedy
commissione *n.f.* commission
compagno *n.m.* partner
comparire *v.* to appear
compartimento *n.m.* compartment
compiacere *v.* to please
compitare *v.* to spell
compleanno *n.m.* birthday
compositore *n.m.* composer
comprare *v.* to buy
comprensione *n.f.* understanding
comune *adj.* common
comunque *adv.* however
con *prep.* with
concentrarsi *v.ref.* to concentrate
concernere *v.* to regard
concerto *n.m.* concert
conchiglia *n.f.* shell
condividere *v.* to share
condurre *v.* to lead

confermare *v.* to confirm
confusione *n.f.* mess, confusion
congresso *n.m.* congress
coniglio *n.m.* rabbit
conoscenza *n.f.* acquaintance
conoscere *v.* to meet, to know
consegnare *v.* to deliver
conseguenza *n.f.* consequence
consigliare *v.* to advise
consiglio *n.m.* advice
contadino *n.m.* farmer, peasant
contante *n.m.* cash
contatto *n.m.* contact
contemporaneo *adj.* contemporary
contenere *v.* to contain
contento *adj.* glad
conto *n.m.* bill
contraccettivo *n.m.* contraceptive
contratto *n.m.* contract
contro *prep.* against
controllare *v.* to check
controllo *n.m.* control
convento *n.m.* convent
conversare *v.* to talk, to chat
conversazione *n.f.* talk, chat
convertire *v.* to convert
coperta *n.f.* blanket
coppa *n.f.* cup
coraggio *n.m.* courage
coraggioso *adj.* brave, courageous
cordoglio *n.m.* grief
corrente *n.f.* current
correre *v.* to run
corsa *n.f.* run
cortese *adj.* kind
corto *adj.* short
cosa *n.f.* thing
coscia *n.f.* thigh
così *adv.* so, thus

costare *v.* to cost
costipato *adj.* constipated
costituzione *n.f.* constitution
costola *n.f.* rib
costoso *adj.* expensive
costruire *v.* to build
costume *n.m.* bathing suit, costume
cotone *n.m.* cotton
crampo *n.m.* cramp
cravatta *n.f.* necktie
credere *v.* to believe
credito *n.m.* credit
crema *n.f.* cream
crepuscolo *n.m.* dusk
crescere *v.* to grow
criminale *adj.* criminal
crisi *n.f.* crisis
cristallo *n.m.* crystal
croce *n.f.* cross
crudo *adj.* raw
cucchiaino *n.m.* teaspoon
cucchiaio *n.m.* spoon
cucina *n.f.* kitchen
cucinare *v.* to cook
cucire *v.* to sew
cugino *n.m.* cousin
cuoco *n.m.* chef, cook
cuore *n.m.* heart
curva *n.f.* bend
cuscino *n.m.* pillow

D

da *prep.* from, since
danaro, denaro *n.m.* money
danneggiare *v.* to damage
danno *n.m.* damage

dare *v.* to give
data *n.f.* date
dattero *n.m.* date (fruit)
davvero *adv.* indeed
debito *n.m.* debt
debole *adj.* weak
debolezza *n.f.* weakness
decaffeinato *adj.* caffeine-free, decaffeinated
decidere *v.* to decide
decimo *adj.* tenth
decisione *n.f.* decision
decorazione *n.f.* decoration
dedicare *v.* to devote
delicato *adj.* delicate
delizioso *adj.* delicious
deludente *adj.* disappointing
delusione *n.f.* disappointment
denso *adj.* dense
dente *n.m.* tooth (*pl.* teeth)
dentifricio *n.m.* toothpaste
dentista *n.m.* dentist
dentro *prep., adv.* inside
deodorante *n.m., adj.* deodorant
deposito *n.m.* deposit
descrivere *v.* to describe
descrizione *n.f.* description
destinazione *n.f.* destination
deteinato *adj.* caffeine-free tea
detestare *v.* to detest, to loathe
deviazione *n.f.* detour
di *prep.* of
diabete diabetes
diabetico *adj.* diabetic
diamante *n.m.* diamond
diarrea *n.f.* diarrhea
dicembre *n.m.* December
dieta *n.f.* diet
dietetico *adj.* dietetic
dietro (a) *prep.* behind

difendere *v.* to defend
differenza *n.f.* difference
difficile *adj.* difficult
difficoltà *n.f.* difficulty
digerire *v.* to digest
digestione *n.f.* digestion
digitare *v.* to dial
dimenticare *v.* to forget
dio *n.m.* god
dipendere *v.* to depend
dipingere *v.* to paint
dire *v.* to say
diretto *adj.* direct
direttore *n.m.* director, conductor
direzione *n.f.* direction
diritto *n.m.* right
discorso *n.m.* speech
disdire *v.* to cancel
disfare *v.* to unpack
disgustoso *adj.* disgusting
disobbedire *v.* to disobey
disoccupato *adj.* unemployed
disonesto *adj.* dishonest
dispari *adj.* odd
dispensare *v.* to exempt; to deal out
disperato *adj.* desperate
dispiacere *n.m.* sorrow
distanza *n.f.* distance
distruggere *v.* to destroy
disturbare *v.* to disturb
dito *n.m.* finger
ditta *n.f.* firm
diventare *v.* to become
divertente *adj.* enjoyable, funny
divertimento *n.m.* fun
divertirsi *v.* to enjoy oneself
divorziare *v.* to divorce
divorziato *adj.* divorced
divorzio *n.m.* divorce

dizionario *n.m.* dictionary
doccia *n.f.* shower
documentazione *n.f.* documentation
documento *n.m.* document
dogana *n.f.* customs *pl.*
dolce *n.m.* cake; *adj.* sweet
dolci *(pl.) n.m.* sweets
dolere *v.* to ache
dollaro *n.m.* dollar
dolore *n.m.* ache, pain
domanda *n.f.* question
domani *adv.* tomorrow
domenica *n.f.* Sunday
domestica *n.f.* housekeeper
donna *n.f.* woman
dopo *adv.* after
doppio *adj.* double
dorato *adj.* golden
dormire *v.* to sleep
dormitorio *n.m.* dormitory
dottore *n.m.* doctor
dottrina *n.f.* doctrine
dove *adv.* where
dovere *n.m.* duty
dovere *v.* must, to have to
dozzina *n.f.* dozen
dritto *adj., adv.* straight
droga *n.f.* drug
dubbio *n.m.* doubt
dubitare *v.* to doubt
durante *prep.* during
durare *v.* to last
durata *n.f.* duration, length
duro *adj.* hard

E

e *conj.* and
ebraico *adj.* Jewish, Hebrew

ebreo *n.m.* Jew
eccellente *adj.* excellent
eccezionale *adj.* exceptional
eccezione *n.f.* exception
eccitato *adj.* excited
edificio *n.m.* building
educato *adj.* polite
egli *pron.* he
egoista *adj.* egotistical, selfish
elefante *n.m.* elephant
eleggere *v.* to elect
elettricità *n.f.* electricity
elettrico *adj.* electric
elettronico *adj.* electronic
elevato *adj.* elevated, high
elezione *n.f.* election
elicottero *n.m.* helicopter
elogiare *v.* to praise
emergenza *n.f.* emergency
emigrazione *n.f.* emigration
energia *n.f.* energy
enorme *adj.* huge
entrambi *adj., adv.* both
entrare *v.* to enter
entusiasta *adj.* enthusiastic
epilettico *adj.* epileptic
equilibrio *n.m.* balance
equipaggiamento *n.m.* equipment
erba *n.f.* grass
erboristeria *n.f.* herbshop
eredità *n.f.* heritage, legacy, inheritance
ereditare *v.* to inherit
erto *adj.* thick
esaurimento *n.m.* exhaustion, breakdown
esausto *adj.* exhausted
escursione *n.f.* excursion, trip
esempio *n.m.* example
esercitarsi *v.ref.* to exercise

esercizio *n.m.* exercise
esibirsi *v.ref.* to perform
esibizione *n.f.* performance
esigenza *n.f.* demand
esigere *v.* to demand
esilio *n.m.* exile
esistenza *n.f.* existence, being
esperienza *n.f.* experience
esperto *n.m.* expert
espresso *adj.* express
esprimere *v.* to express
essere *v.* to be
Est *n.* East
estate *n.f.* summer
estinguere *v.* to extinguish
estremità *n.f.* extremity, end
esultare *v.* to rejoice
età *n.f.* age
eternità *n.f.* eternity
etichetta *n.f.* label
etichettare *v.* to label
Europa *n.f.* Europe
europeo *adj.* European
evadere *v.* to escape
evidente *adj.* evident

F

fa *adv.* ago
facile *adj.* easy
fagiolo *n.m.* bean
falco *n.m.* falcon
falla *n.f.* flaw
falso *adj.* false
fame *n.f.* hunger
famiglia *n.f.* family
famoso *adj.* famous
fanatico *adj.* fanatic

fango *n.m.* mud
fantastico *adj.* fantastic
fare *v.* to do, to make
farfalla *n.f.* butterfly
farina *n.f.* flour
farmacia *n.f.* pharmacy
faro *n.m.* headlight
fasciatura *n.f.* bandage
fattoria *n.f.* farm
fattura *n.f.* invoice
favola *n.f.* tale
favore *n.m.* favor
fazzoletto *n.m.* handkerchief
febbraio *n.m.* February
febbre *n.f.* fever
fede *n.f.* faith
fedeltà *n.f.* fidelity, faithfulness
federa *n.f.* pillowcase
fegato *n.m.* liver
felice *adj.* happy
felicità *n.f.* happiness
femminile *adj.* feminine
ferire *v.* to hurt, to wound
ferita *n.f.* wound, scar, injury
ferito *adj.* injured
fermare *v.* to stop
fermata *n.f.* (bus, train) stop
fermentare *v.* to ferment
fermo *adj.* still, steady
ferramenta *n.m.* locksmith
ferro *n.m.* iron
ferrovia *n.f.* railroad
festa *n.f.* feast
festività *n.f.* festivity, holiday
fiammifero *n.m.* match
fico *n.m.* fig
fidanzata *n.f.* fiancée
fidanzato *n.m.* fiancé
fiducia *n.f.* confidence, trust

figlia *n.f.* daughter
figlio *n.m.* son
fila *n.f.* queue, line
filetto *n.m.* fillet
filiale *n.f.* branch
filo *n.m.* thread
filosofia *n.f.* philosophy
filtro *n.m.* filter
finalmente *adv.* finally
finanze *(pl.)* *n.f.* finances
finché *conj.* until
fine *n.f.* end
finestra *n.f.* window
fingere *v.* to pretend
finire *v.* to finish
fiocco *n.m.* ribbon
fioraio *n.m.* florist
fiore *n.m.* flower
firma *n.f.* signature
fischiare *v.* to whistle
fisica *n.f.* physics
fissare *v.* to fix
fiume *n.m.* river
flanella *n.f.* flannel
flessibile *adj.* flexible
foglia *n.f.* leaf (*pl.* leaves)
fondazione *n.f.* foundation
fondo *n.m.* bottom
fontana *n.f.* fountain
forbici *(pl.)* *n.f.* scissors
forchetta *n.f.* fork
foresta *n.f.* forest
forestale *adj.* forestal; *n.* forester
forma *n.f.* shape, form
formaggio *n.m.* cheese
formica *n.f.* ant
fornaio *n.m.* baker
forno *n.m.* oven
forse *adv.* maybe, perhaps

forte *adj.* strong
fortezza *n.f.* fortress
fortuna *n.f.* fortune, luck
forza *n.f.* force
forzare *v.* to force
fotocopia *n.f.* photocopy
fotografia *n.f.* photograph
fra, tra *prep.* between
fragile *adj.* fragile
fragola *n.f.* strawberry
fraintendere *v.* to misunderstand
fraintendimento *n.m.* misunderstanding
francescano *adj.* Franciscan
francese *adj.* French
Francia *n.f.* France
francobollo *n.m.* stamp
frase *n.f.* phrase, sentence
fratello *n.m.* brother
frattura *n.f.* fracture
freddo *adj.* cold
freno *n.m.* brake
fresco *adj.* fresh
fretta *n.f.* hurry
friggere *v.* to fry
frigorifero *n.m.* fridge
frittata *n.f.* omelette
fritto *adj.* fried
frivolo *adj.* frivolous
fronte *n.f.* forehead
frutta *n.f.* fruit
fruttivendolo *n.m.* greengrocer
fuga *n.f.* escape
fulmine *n.m.* lightning
fumare *v.* to smoke
fumatore *n.m.* smoker
fumo *n.m.* smoke
funerale *n.m.* funeral
fungo *n.m.* mushroom
funzionare *v.* to function

fuoco *n.m.* fire
fuori *prep.* out
furioso *adj.* furious
furto *n.m.* robbery
fusibile *n.m.* fuse
futuro *n.m.* future

G

gaio *adj.* gay, merry
gallo *n.m.* cock
gamba *n.f.* leg
gamberetto *n.m.* shrimp
garantire *v.* to ensure
garanzia *n.f.* guarantee
gastrite *n.f.* gastritis
gatto *n.m.* cat
gelatina *n.f.* jelly
gelato *n.m.* ice cream; *adj.* frozen
gelosia *n.f.* jealousy
geloso *adj.* jealous
gemelli *(pl.)* *n.m.* twins
gemello *adj.* twin
generale *n.m., adj.* general
generalmente *adv.* generally
genero *n.m.* son-in-law
generosità *n.f.* generosity
genitali *(pl.)* *n.m.* genitals
genitori *(pl.)* *n.m.* parents
gennaio *n.m.* January
gente *n.f.* people *pl.*
gentilezza *n.f.* kindness
genuino *adj.* genuine
Germania *n.f.* Germany
gettare *v.* to throw
ghiaccio *n.m.* ice
ghiandola *n.f.* gland
già *adv.* already

giacchetta *n.f.* jacket
giallo *adj.* yellow
Giappone *n.m.* Japan
giapponese *n.m., adj.* Japanese
giardino *n.m.* garden
ginecologo *n.m.* gynecologist
ginnastica *n.f.* gymnastics
ginocchio *(pl. ginocchia)* *n.m.* knee
giocare *v.* to play (a game)
giocattolo *n.m.* toy
gioielleria *n.f.* jewelry
gioiello *n.m.* jewel
giorno *n.m.* day
giovane *adj.* young
giovanotto *n.m.* lad; young man
giovedì *n.m.* Thursday
gioventù *n.f.* youth
girare *v.* to turn
giù *adv., prep.* below, down
giudicare *v.* to judge
giudice *n.m.* judge
giudizio *n.m.* judgment
giugno *n.m.* June
giuoco *n.m.* game
giurare *v.* to swear
giustizia *n.f.* justice
giusto *adj.* just, right
globo *n.m.* globe
goccia *n.f.* drop
gola *n.f.* throat
gonna *n.f.* skirt
governo *n.m.* government
grado *n.m.* extent, grade
grammo *n.m.* gram
Gran Bretagna *n.f.* Great Britain
granchio *n.m.* crab
grande *adj.* big
grano *n.m.* cereal

grasso *n.m., adj.* fat
gratuito *adj.* free, gratis
gravida *adj.* pregnant
Grazie! *interj.* Thank you!
grazioso *adj.* lovely, pretty
Grecia *n.f.* Greece
greco *n.m., adj.* Greek
grigio *adj.* grey
grotta *n.f.* cave
gruppo *n.m.* group
guadagnare *v.* to earn
guanto *n.m.* glove
guardare *v.* to look, to watch
guardaroba *n.f.* wardrobe
guarigione *n.f.* recovery
guarire *v.* to recover
guasto *n.m.* failure
guerra *n.f.* war
gufo *n.m.* owl
guida *n.f.* guide, guidebook
guidare *v.* to drive
guscio *n.m.* shell

I

idea *n.f.* idea
identità *n.f.* identity
idiota *n.m., adj.* idiot
idratante *adj.* moistening, moisturizing
ieri *n.m., adv.* yesterday
illegale *adj.* unlawful
illegittimo *adj.* illegitimate
illuminare *v.* to light
imbarazzare *v.* to embarrass
imbarazzato *adj.* ashamed, embarrassed
imbarazzo *n.m.* embarrassment
imbucare *v.* to mail

immaginare *v.* to imagine
immagine *n.f.* image
immediatamente *adv.* immediately
immorale *adj.* immoral
immortale *adj.* immortal
immunizzare *v.* to immunize
immunizzazione *n.f.* immunization
imparare *v.* to learn
impaziente *adj.* impatient
impazzire *v.* to go crazy, to lose one's head
impegno *n.m.* engagement, commitment
impermeabile *n.m.* raincoat; *adj.* waterproof
impersonale *adj.* impersonal
impopolare *adj.* unpopular
importante *adj.* important
impossibile *adj.* impossible
impregnare *v.* to saturate
impressione *n.f.* impression
improvviso *adj.* sudden
in *prep.* in
inadatto *adj.* improper, unfit
inaffidabile *adj.* unreliable
incapace *adj.* incapable
incerto *adj.* uncertain
incidente *n.m.* accident, incident
includere *v.* to include
incomprensibile *adj.* incomprehensible
incontrare *v.* to meet
incontro *n.m.* meeting
incosciente *adj.* unconscious; reckless
incredibile *adj.* incredible, unbelievable
incrementare *v.* to increase
incremento *n.m.* increase
incrocio *n.m.* crossing, intersection
indietro *adv.* back, behind
indifferente *adj.* indifferent
indigestione *n.f.* indigestion
indipendente *adj.* independent
indipendenza *n.f.* independence

indirizzo *n.m.* address
industria *n.f.* factory
infastidire *v.* to annoy
infatti *conj.* actually
infedele *adj.* untrue
infelice *adj.* unhappy
infelicità *n.f.* unhappiness
inferiore *adj.* inferior
infermiera *n.f.* nurse
inferno *n.m.* hell
infezione *n.f.* infection
infiammabile *adj.* inflammable
infiammazione *n.f.* inflammation
informazione *n.f.* information
infrazione *n.f.* infraction
ingegnere *n.m.* engineer
inginocchiarsi *v.* to kneel
ingiusto *adj.* unjust
inglese *adj.* English, British
ingoiare *v.* to swallow
ingorgo *n.m.* obstruction, traffic jam
ingratitudine *n.f.* ingratitude
ingresso *n.m.* entrance
iniezione *n.f.* injection
iniziare *v.* to begin, to start
inizio *n.m.* beginning
inno *n.m.* anthem, hymn
innocente *adj.* innocent
inquietudine *n.f.* unrest
inquinato *adj.* polluted
insalata *n.f.* salad
insegnante *n.m.* teacher
insegnare *v.* to teach
insetto *n.m.* insect
insieme *adv.* together
insoddisfatto *adj.* dissatisfied
insolito *adj.* unusual
insonne *adj.* sleepless
instabile *adj.* unstable

insultare *v.* to insult
insulto *n.m.* insult
intelligente *adj.* clever, intelligent
interessante *adj.* interesting
interessare *v.* to interest
interesse *n.m.* interest
intermezzo *n.m.* intermission
internazionale *adj.* international
intero *adj.* whole
interpretare *v.* to interpret
interprete *n.m.* interpreter
intestino *n.m.* intestines *pl.*
intimo *adj.* underwear
intorno *adv.* around
intrattenimento *n.m.* entertainment
inutile *adj.* useless
invalido *adj.* invalid
invece *adv.* instead (of)
inverno *n.m.* winter
investigare *v.* to investigate
investigazione *n.f.* investigation
investimento *n.m.* investment
investire *v.* to invest
invidiare *v.* to envy
invitare *v.* to invite
invitato *n.m.* guest
invito *n.m.* invitation
io *pron.* I
iodio *n.m.* iodine
ira *n.f.* anger
Irlanda *n.f.* Ireland
irlandese *n.m., adj.* Irish
irragionevole *adj.* unreasonable
irreale *adj.* unreal
irregolare *adj.* irregular
irresponsabile *adj.* irresponsible
irritare *v.* to irritate
iscriversi *v.ref.* to register
iscrizione *n.f.* registration

isola *n.f.* island
ispezione *n.f.* examination
Israele *n.m.* Israel
israeliano *n.m., adj.* Israeli
istituto *n.m.* institute
istruzione *n.f.* education
Italia *n.f.* Italy
italiano *n.m., adj.* Italian

L

là *adv.* there
labbro *(pl. labbra)* *n.m.* lip
laccio *n.m.* lace
lacrima *n.f.* tear
ladro *n.m.* robber, thief
lago *n.m.* lake
lampada *n.f.* lamp
lampadina *n.f.* bulb
lampone *n.m.* raspberry
lana *n.f.* wool
lanterna *n.f.* lantern
lardo *n.m.* lard
larghezza *n.f.* width
largo *adj.* large
lasciare *v.* to leave, to let
lassativo *n.m., adj.* laxative
lato *n.m.* side
latte *n.m.* milk
lattuga *n.f.* lettuce
lavabo *n.m.* basin
lavagna *n.f.* blackboard
lavanderia *n.f.* dry cleaner, laundry
lavandino *n.m.* sink
lavare *v.* to wash
lavorare *v.* to work
lavoro *n.m.* work
legge *n.f.* law

leggere *v.* to read
leggero *adj.* light
legno *n.m.* wood
lente *n.f.* lens
lenticchia *n.f.* lentil
lenzuolo *n.m.* sheet
leone *n.m.* lion
lesso *adj.* boiled
lettera *n.f.* letter
letteratura *n.f.* literature
letto *n.m.* bed
levatrice *n.f.* midwife
lezione *n.f.* lesson
libbra *n.f.* pound
liberazione *n.f.* liberation
libero *adj.* free
libertà *n.f.* freedom
libreria *n.f.* bookstore
libro *n.m.* book
lievito *n.m.* yeast
limonata *n.f.* lemonade
limone *n.m.* lemon
linea *n.f.* line
lingua *n.f.* language, tongue
liquido *n.m., adj.* liquid
liquore *n.m.* liqueur, spirits
liscio *adj.* smooth
litigare *v.* to quarrel
litro *n.m.* liter
livido *n.m.* bruise
locale *adj.* local
località *n.f.* locality, place
lontano *adj.* far
lotta *n.f.* fight
lotteria *n.f.* lottery
lozione *n.f.* lotion
luce *n.f.* light
lucertola *n.f.* lizard

luglio *n.m.* July
lugubre *adj.* mournful
luna *n.f.* moon
lunedì *n.m.* Monday
lunghezza *n.f.* length
lungo *adj.* long
luogo *n.m.* place
lupo *n.m.* wolf
lusso *n.m.* luxury

M

ma *conj.* but
macchia *n.f.* spot
macchiato *adj.* stained
macchina *n.f.* car
macellaio *n.m.* butcher
madre *n.f.* mother
maggio *n.m.* May
maggioranza *n.f.* majority
maglione *n.m.* pullover, sweater
magnifico *adj.* great, magnificent
magro *adj.* slim
mai *adv.* never
maiale *n.m.* pig
malato *adj.* sick
malattia *n.f.* disease, illness, sickness
malgrado *conj.* although; *prep.* despite
malsano *adj.* unhealthy
mancanza *n.f.* lack
mancare *v.* to lack, to miss
mancia *n.f.* tip
mandarino *n.m.* tangerine
mandorla *n.f.* almond
mangiare *v.* to eat
manica *n.f.* sleeve
manifattura *n.f.* handmade

maniglia *n.f.* handle
mano *n.f.* hand
mantenere *v.* to maintain
manuale *n.m., adj.* handbook, manual
manzo *n.m.* beef
marciapiede *n.m.* sidewalk
marcio *adj.* rotten
mare *n.m.* sea
marea *n.f.* tide
margarina *n.f.* margarine
marinato *adj.* marinated
marito *n.m.* husband
marrone *adj.* brown
martedì *n.m.* Tuesday
martello *n.m.* hammer
marzo *n.m.* March
mascella *n.f.* jaw
matematica *n.f.* mathematics
materasso *n.m.* mattress
materiale *n.m., adj.* material
matita *n.f.* pencil
matrimonio *n.m.* wedding
mattino *n.m.* morning
matto *n.m.* madman; *adj.* mad
meccanico *adj.* mechanic
medicina *n.f.* medicine
medio *adj.* middle, medium
medioevo *n.m.* Middle Ages
Mediterraneo *n.m., adj.* Mediterranean
mela *n.f.* apple
melanzana *n.f.* eggplant
melone *n.m.* melon
membro *n.m.* member
memoria *n.f.* memory
mendicante *n.m.* beggar
meno *adj., adv.* less
mente *n.f.* mind
mentire *v.* to lie

mentre *adv.* meanwhile
menzogna *n.f.* lie
meraviglia *n.f.* wonder
meraviglioso *adj.* wonderful
mercato *n.m.* market
merce *n.f.* goods *pl.*
mercoledì *n.m.* Wednesday
meridionale *adj.* southern
merluzzo *n.m.* cod
meschino *adj.* mean
mese *n.m.* month
messa *n.f.* mass
messaggio *n.m.* message
metà *n.f.* half
metro *n.m.* meter
mezzanotte *n.f.* midnight
mezzo *n.m.* means
miele *n.m.* honey
miglioramento *n.m.* improvement
migliorare *v.* to improve
milione *n.m.* million
minaccia *n.f.* threat
minacciare *v.* to threaten
minerale *n.m., adj.* mineral
minestra *n.f.* soup
minorenne *n.m.* minor
minuto *n.m.* minute
mischiare *v.* to mix
miseria *n.f.* misery
missile *n.m.* missile
mistero *n.m.* mystery
misura *n.f.* measure; size
misurare *v.* to measure
misurazione *n.f.* measurement
mobile *n.m.* furniture
moderno *adj.* modern
modestia *n.f.* modesty
moglie *n.f.* wife

molti *adj., pron.* many
molto *adj., adv.* much
momento *n.m.* moment
monaco *n.m.* monk
monastero *n.m.* monastery
mondo *n.m.* world
moneta *n.f.* coin
montagna *n.f.* mountain
monumento *n.m.* monument
morale *n.m., n.f.* moral
morbido *adj.* soft
morbillo *n.m.* measles
morire *v.* to die
morte *n.f.* death
morto *n.m., adj.* dead
mosca *n.f.* fly
moschea *n.f.* mosque
mostarda *n.f.* mustard
mostrare *v.* to show
mostro *n.m.* monster
motocicletta *n.f.* motorcycle
motore *n.m.* engine
movimento *n.m.* movement
multa *n.f.* penalty, fine
muovere *v.* to move
muscolo *n.m.* muscle
museo *n.m.* museum
musica *n.f.* music
musicista *n.m.* player, musician
mutande *(pl.) n.f.* panties
muto *adj.* dumb, mute
mutuo *adj.* mutual

N

nascita *n.f.* birth
nascondere *v.* to hide

naso *n.m.* nose
nastro *n.m.* tape
Natale *n.m.* Christmas
natura *n.f.* nature
nausea *n.f.* nausea
navigare *v.* to sail
nazionale *adj.* national
nazione *n.f.* nation
né...né *adj., adv.* neither...nor
nebbia *n.f.* fog
nebbioso *adj.* foggy
necessario *adj.* necessary
necessità *n.f.* necessity
negativo *adj.* negative
negoziante *n.m.* shopkeeper
negozio *n.m.* shop, store
nemico *n.m.* enemy
nero *n.m., adj.* black
nervo *n.m.* nerve
nervoso *adj.* nervous
nessuno *pron.* nobody
neve *n.f.* snow
nevicare *v.* to snow
nevrotico *adj.* neurotic
niente *pron.* nothing
nipote *n.f.* granddaughter; *n.m.* grandson
nipote *n.m.* nephew; *n.f.* niece
nocciuola *n.f.* hazelnut
noce *n.f.* nut, walnut
noia *n.f.* boredom
noioso *adj.* boring
nolo *n.m.* freight
nome *n.m.* name
nonna *n.f.* grandmother
nonno *n.m.* grandfather
Nord *n.m.* North
nordico *adj.* northern
normale *adj.* normal

notare *v.* to notice
notevole *adj.* impressive
notiziario *n.m.* news *pl.*
notte *n.f.* night
novembre *n.m.* November
nudo *adj.* naked
numero *n.m.* number
nuotare *v.* to swim
nuotatore *n.m.* swimmer
nuovo *adj.* new
nutrimento *n.m.* nourishment
nutrire *v.* to nourish, to feed
nuvoloso *adj.* cloudy

O

obiettare *v.* to object
oca *n.f.* goose (*pl.* geese)
occasione *n.f.* chance, occasion
occhiali *(pl.) n.m.* eyeglasses
occhio *n.m.* eye
occidentale *adj.* western
occupare *v.* to occupy
occupato *adj.* busy, occupied
oceano *n.m.* ocean
oculista *n.m.* oculist
odiare *v.* to hate
odio *n.m.* hatred
odioso *adj.* obnoxious
odorare *v.* to smell
odore *n.m.* smell
offendere *v.* to offend
offerta *n.f.* offer
offesa *n.f.* offense
offrire *v.* to offer
oggetto *n.m.* object
oggi *n.m., adv.* today

ogni *adj.* each, every
olfatto *n.m.* smell
olio *n.m.* oil
oliva *n.f.* olive
ombra *n.f.* shadow
ombrello *n.m.* umbrella
onda *n.f.* wave
onesto *adj.* honest
onore *n.m.* honor
opera *n.f.* opera; deed
operaio *n.m.* worker
operatore *n.m.* operator
operazione *n.f.* operation
opinione *n.f.* opinion
opportunità *n.f.* opportunity
opportuno *adj.* proper
opposto *adj.* opposite
ora *n.f.* hour
ora *adv.* now
orale *adj.* oral
ordinare *v.* to order
ordinario *adj.* ordinary
ordine *n.m.* order
orecchio *n.m.* ear
orfano *adj.* orphan
organizzare *v.* to organize
organizzazione *n.f.* organization
orgoglio *n.m.* pride
orgoglioso *adj.* proud
orientale *adj.* eastern
originare *v.* to originate
oriundo *n.m., adj.* native
oro *n.m.* gold
orologiaio *n.m.* watchmaker
orologio *n.m.* clock, watch
orrore *n.m.* horror
ospedale *n.m.* hospital
ospite *n.m.* guest
ossigeno *n.m.* oxygen

osso *(pl. ossa) n.m.* bone
ostaggio *n.m.* hostage
ostrica *n.f.* oyster
ottenere *v.* to obtain
ottobre *n.m.* October
ovale *adj.* oval
Ovest *n.m.* West
ovunque *adv.* everywhere
ovvio *adj.* obvious

P

pacco *n.m.* package, parcel
pace *n.f.* peace
Pacifico *n.m.* Pacific
pacifico *adj.* peaceful
padre *n.m.* father
paesaggio *n.m.* landscape
pagamento *n.m.* payment
pagare *v.* to pay
pagina *n.f.* page
paglia *n.f.* straw
paio *n.m.* pair
palazzo *n.m.* palace
pallido *adj.* pale
pallone *n.m.* ball
palma *n.f.* palm
palpitare *v.* to palpitate
palpitazione *n.m.* palpitation
pancetta *n.f.* bacon
panchina *n.f.* bench
pane *n.m.* bread
panfilo *n.m.* yacht
panico *n.m.* panic
panino *n.m.* sandwich
panna *n.f.* whipped cream
pantaloni *(pl.) n.m.* trousers
paonazzo *adj.* purple

paradiso *n.m.* heaven, paradise
paralisi *n.f.* paralysis
paralizzare *v.* to paralyze
parasole *n.m.* parasol; sunshade
parco *n.m.* park, parking
parente *n.m.* relative
parete *n.f.* wall
parlamento *n.m.* parliament
parlare *v.* to speak
parola *n.f.* word
parrocchia *n.f.* parish
parrucchiere *n.m.* hairdresser
parte *n.f.* part
partecipare *v.* to participate
partecipazione *n.f.* participation
partenza *n.f.* departure
partire *v.* to depart, to leave
Pasqua *n.f.* Easter
passaggio *n.m.* passage
passaporto *n.m.* passport
passare *v.* to pass
passato *n.m.* past
passeggero *n.m., adj.* passenger
passeggiata *n.f.* walk, stroll
passero *n.m.* sparrow
passione *n.f.* passion
passo *n.m.* pace, step
pasticceria *n.f.* pastry
pastiglia *n.f.* tablet
pasto *n.m.* meal
patata *n.f.* potato
patente *n.f.* (driver's) license
pattinare *v.* to skate
pattuglia *n.f.* patrol
paura *n.f.* fear
pavimento *n.m.* floor
paziente *n.m., adj.* patient
pazienza *n.f.* patience
pazzo *adj.* insane, crazy

peccare *v.* to sin
peccato *n.m.* sin
pecora *n.f.* sheep
pedale *n.m.* pedal
peggiorare *v.* to worsen
pelle *n.f.* leather, skin
pelliccia *n.f.* fur
pellicola *n.f.* film
pena *n.f.* pain, pity
pendio *n.m.* hillside
pene *n.m.* penis
penna *n.f.* pen
pennello *n.m.* paintbrush
pensare *v.* to think
pensione *n.f.* guesthouse; pension
pepe *n.m.* pepper
per *prep.* for
pera *n.f.* pear
percentuale *n.f.* percentage
perché *conj.* because
perché *adv., conj.* why
perciò *adv.* therefore
percorso *n.m.* route
perdere *v.* to lose
perdita *n.f.* loss
perdonare *v.* to forgive
perfetto *adj.* perfect
pericolo *n.m.* danger
pericoloso *adj.* dangerous
periodo *n.m.* period
perire *v.* to perish
perla *n.f.* pearl
permanente *adj.* permanent
permanenza *n.f.* stay
permesso *n.m.* permission, permit
permettere *v.* to allow, to permit
persiana *n.f.* blind (window)

persino *adv.* even
persistente *adj.* persistent
persistenza *n.f.* persistence
persistere *v.* to persist
personale *adj.* personal
pesante *adj.* heavy
pesare *v.* to weigh
pesca *n.f.* peach
pesca *n.f.* fishing
pesce *n.m.* fish
peso *n.m.* weight
petrolio *n.m.* petroleum
pettegolezzo *n.m.* gossip
petto *n.m.* breast, chest
pezzo *n.m.* piece
piacere *v.int.* to like
piacere *n.m.* pleasure
piacevole *adj.* agreeable
piangere *v.* to cry
pianificare *v.* to plan
piano *n.m.* plan
pianoforte *n.m.* piano
pianta *n.f.* plant
piantare *v.* to plant
piatto *n.m.* dish; plate
piazza *n.f.* square
piazzare *v.* to place
piccione *n.m.* pigeon
picco *n.m.* peak
piccolo *adj.* little, small
piede *n.m.* foot (*pl.* feet)
pieno *adj.* full
pietà *n.f.* mercy
pietra *n.f.* rock, stone
pigro *adj.* lazy
pillola *n.f.* pill
pilota *n.m.* pilot
pinguino *n.m.* penguin

pino *n.m.* pine tree
pioggia *n.f.* rain
piombo *n.m.* lead
piovere *v.* to rain
piscina *n.f.* swimming pool
pisello *n.m.* pea
pistola *n.f.* gun
pittore *n.m.* painter
più *pron., adv., adj.* more
piuttosto *adv.* quite, rather
plastica *n.f.* plastic
poco *pron., adj., adv.* a bit, little, few
poesia *n.f.* poem, poetry
poi *adv.* then
polacco *n.m., adj.* Polish
polipo *n.m.* octopus
polizia *n.f.* police
poliziotto *n.m.* policeman
pollame *n.m.* poultry
pollo *n.m.* chicken
polmoni *(pl.) n.m.* lungs
polmonite *n.f.* pneumonia
Polonia *n.f.* Poland
polpetta *n.f.* meatball
polso *n.m.* wrist, pulse
polvere *n.f.* dust
pomeriggio *n.m.* afternoon
pomodoro *n.m.* tomato
pompa *n.f.* pump
pompelmo *n.m.* grapefruit
ponte *n.m.* bridge
popolare *adj.* popular
popolo *n.m.* populace, people
porcellana *n.f.* porcelain
porco *n.m.* pork
porta *n.f.* door
portafoglio *n.m.* wallet
portare *v.* to bring

portiere *n.m.* porter
porzione *n.f.* portion
posacenere *n.m.* ashtray
possesso *n.m.* possession
possibile *adj.* possible
possibilità *n.f.* possibility
posta *n.f.* post office, mail
posta aerea *n.f.* airmail
posteggio *n.m.* park
posteriore *adj.* rear
potere *v.* to be able to, can
potere *n.m.* power
povero *adj.* poor
povertà *n.f.* poverty
pozzo *n.m.* well
pranzare *v.* to have lunch
pranzo *n.m.* lunch
precauzione *n.f.* precaution
preciso *adj.* precise
preferito *adj.* favorite
pregare *v.* to pray
preistorico *adj.* prehistoric
prendere *v.* to take
prenotare *v.* to reserve
prenotazione *n.f.* reservation
preoccuparsi *v.ref.* to worry
preoccupazione *n.f.* worry
preparare *v.* to prepare
prescrivere *v.* to prescribe
presentare *v.* to introduce; to present
presentazione *n.f.* introduction
preservativo *n.m.* condom
pressione *n.f.* blood pressure; pressure
prestare *v.* to lend
presto *adj., adv.* early, soon
prete *n.m.* priest
prezzemolo *n.m.* parsley
prezzo *n.m.* price

prigione *n.f.* jail, prison
prima *adv., prep.* before, earlier
primavera *n.f.* spring
primo *adj.* first
principale *adj.* main
principe *n.m.* prince
principessa *n.f.* princess
principiante *n.m.* beginner
privato *adj.* private
probabile *adj.* probably
problema *n.m.* problem
processo *n.m.* process
produrre *v.* to produce
produzione *n.f.* production
professione *n.f.* profession
professore *n.m.* professor
profitto *n.m.* profit
profondo *adj.* deep
profumo *n.m.* perfume
programma *n.m.* program
proibire *v.* to forbid, to prohibit
proibito *adj.* forbidden
promessa *n.f.* promise
pronto *adj.* ready
pronuncia *n.f.* pronunciation
proposta *n.f.* proposal
proprietà *n.f.* ownership
proprietario *n.m.* owner
prosciutto *n.m.* ham
prossimo *adj., adv.* next
proteggere *v.* to protect
protezione *n.f.* protection
prova *n.f.* proof
provare *v.* to try, to prove
proverbio *n.m.* proverb
provvista *n.f.* stock
prudere *v.* to hitch
prugna *n.f.* plum

prurito *n.m.* itch
pubblicità *n.f.* advertisement
pubblico *n.m.* audience; *adj.* public
pulce *n.f.* flea market
pulire *v.* to clean
pulito *adj.* clean
punizione *n.f.* punishment
puzzare *v.* to stink

Q

quaderno *n.m.* notebook
quadro *n.m.* painting
qualche *adj., pron.* some
qualcosa *pron.* something
qualcuno *pron.* someone
qualifica *n.f.* qualification
qualificare *v.* to qualify
qualificato *adj.* qualified
qualità *n.f.* quality
quando *adv., conj.* when
quantità *n.f.* quantity
quartiere *n.m.* quarter
quasi *adv.* almost, near
quello *adj., pron.* that
questione *n.f.* question, issue
qui *adv.* here
quieto *adj.* quiet
quintetto *n.m.* quintet
quotidiano *n.m.* newspaper; *adj.* daily

R

rabbino *n.m.* rabbi
raccogliere *v.* to pick (up)
raccolto *n.m.* harvest
raccomandare *v.* to recommend

raccomandazione *n.f.* recommendation
raccontare *v.* to tell
radere *v.* to shave
radiatore *n.m.* radiator
raffinato *adj.* fine
raffreddore *n.m.* cold (illness), flu
ragazza *n.f.* girl
ragazzo *n.m.* boy
raggi x *(pl.) n.m.* X rays
ragione *n.f.* reason
rame *n.m.* copper
ramo *n.m.* branch
rana *n.f.* frog
rapido *adj.* quick, fast
rappresentante *n.m.* representative
raramente *adv.* seldom
raro *adj.* rare
rasoio *n.m.* razor
rassomiglianza *n.f.* resemblance
ratto *n.m.* rat
ravanello *n.m.* radish
razza *n.f.* race
razzista *adj.* racist
re *n.m.* king
reale *adj.* royal; real
recinto *n.m.* fence, enclosure
recitare *v.* to act, to play (theater, cinema, etc.)
reclamo *n.m.* complaint
redditizio *adj.* profitable
regalare *v.* to give
regalo *n.m.* gift, present
reggiseno *n.m.* bra
regina *n.f.* queen
regione *n.f.* region
regola *n.f.* rule
regolare *adj.* regular
relativo *adj.* relative
relazione *n.f.* relationship
religione *n.f.* religion

religioso *adj.* religious
rene *n.m.* kidney
reparto *n.m.* department
residenza *n.f.* residence
resistenza *n.f.* resistance
resoconto *n.m.* report
respirare *v.* to breathe
respiro *n.m.* breath
responsabile *adj.* responsible
responsabilità *n.f.* responsibility
restare *v.* to stay, to remain
resto *n.m.* change, rest
reumatismi *(pl.) n.m.* rheumatism *s.*
ricco *adj.* rich
ricerca *n.f.* research
ricercare *v.* to research, to search
ricetta *n.f.* prescription; recipe
ricevere *v.* to receive
ricevitore *n.m.* receiver
ricevuta *n.f.* receipt
ricezione *n.f.* reception
richiedere *v.* to request
richiesta *n.f.* request, demand
riconoscere *v.* to recognize
ricordare *v.* to remember
ricordo *n.m.* recollection
ridere *v.* to laugh
ridicolo *adj.* ridiculous
riduzione *n.f.* reduction
riempire *v.* to fill
rievocare *v.* to recall, to commemorate
rifiutare *v.* to refuse
rifiuti *(pl.) n.m.* garbage *s.*
rifiuto *n.m.* refusal
riflessione *n.f.* reflection
riflettere *v.* to reflect
rifugiato *n.m.* refugee
rifugio *n.m.* refuge, shelter

riguardi (i miei riguardi) *(pl.)* *n.m.* (my) regards
riguardo a *prep.* regarding
rilassarsi *v.ref.* to relax
rimanere *v.* to remain
rimborsare *v.* to refund
rimescolare *v.* to stir
rinforzare *v.* to strengthen
rinfrescarsi *v.ref.* to refresh
ringraziare *v.* to thank
riparare *v.* to repair
ripetere *v.* to repeat
ripieno *n.m., adj.* stuffing, filling
riposare *v.* to rest
riposo *n.m.* rest
ripugnante *adj.* repugnant
risiedere *v.* to reside
riso *n.m.* rice
rispettabile *adj.* respectable
rispettare *v.* to respect
rispetto *n.m.* respect
rispondere *v.* to answer
risposta *n.f.* answer
ristoro *n.m.* refreshment
ristrutturare *v.* to restructure
ritardare *v.* to be late, to delay
ritardo *n.m.* delay
ritirare *v.* to withdraw
ritornare *v.* to return
ritorno *n.m.* return
riunione *n.f.* gathering
riunirsi *v.ref.* to gather
riuscire *v.* to succeed
rivale *n.m.* rival
rivelare *v.* to reveal
rivista *n.f.* magazine
robusto *adj.* tough
romanzo *n.m.* novel
rompere *v.* to break

rosa *n.f.* rose; *adj.* pink
rosario *n.m.* rosary
rossetto *n.m.* lipstick
rosso *adj.* red
rotondo *adj.* round
rotto *adj.* broken
rottura *n.f.* breakdown
rovina *n.f.* ruin
rovinare *v.* to ruin
rovinato *adj.* ruined
rubare *v.* to steal
ruggine *n.f.* rust
rumoroso *adj.* noisy
ruota *n.f.* wheel
ruscello *n.m.* stream
russare *v.* to snore
Russia *n.f.* Russia
russo *n.m., adj.* Russian

S

sabato *n.m.* Saturday
sabbia *n.f.* sand
saggio *adj.* wise
sagra *n.f.* festival
sala *n.f.* hall
salario *n.m.* salary, wages *pl.*
sale *n.m.* salt
salmone *n.m.* salmon
salsiccia *n.f.* sausage
saltare *v.* to jump
salutare *adj.* healthy
salute *n.f.* health
Salute! *interj.* Cheers! Bless You!
saluto *n.m.* greeting
salvare *v.* to save
Salve! *interj.* Hello!
salvia *n.f.* sage

salvo *adj.* safe
sandalo *n.m.* sandal
sangue *n.m.* blood
sanguinare *v.* to bleed
santo *n.m.* saint
sapere *v.* to know
sapone *n.m.* soap
sapore *n.m.* taste
saporito *adj.* tasty
sardina *n.f.* sardine
sarto *n.m.* tailor
sbadigliare *v.* to yawn
sbagliato *adj.* wrong
sbaglio *n.m.* mistake
sbornia *n.f.* drunkenness
scadenza *n.f.* deadline
scaffale *n.m.* shelf
scala *n.f.* staircase
scalino *n.m.* stair
scambiare *v.* to exchange; to mistake
scarafaggio *n.m.* cockroach
scarpa *n.f.* shoe
scatola *n.f.* box
scatoletta *n.f.* can
scegliere *v.* to choose
scelta *n.f.* choice
schedario *n.m.* file
scherzare *v.* to joke
scherzo *n.m.* joke
schiudere *v.* to unfold
sci *(pl.)* *n.m.* skis
sciare *v.* to ski
sciarpa *n.f.* scarf
scienza *n.f.* science
scienziato *n.m.* scientist
scintilla *n.f.* spark
sciocco *adj.* dull
sciopero *n.m.* strike
scivolare *v.* to slide
scoglio *n.m.* cliff

scolaro *n.m.* pupil
scomodo *adj.* uncomfortable
scomparire *v.* to disappear
sconosciuto *adj.* unknown
sconvolgere *v.* to upset
sconvolto *adj.* upset
scopo *n.m.* purpose, goal
scoprire *v.* to discover
scorrere *v.* to flow
scortese *adj.* unkind
Scozia *n.f.* Scotland
scozzese *n.m., adj.* Scottish
scrittore *n.m.* writer
scrivere *v.* to write
scultore *n.m.* sculptor
scultura *n.f.* sculpture
scuola *n.f.* school
scuotere *v.* to shake
scusa *n.f.* excuse
scusare *v.* to excuse
Scusi! *interj.* Sorry!
se *conj.* if
sé *n.m.* self
sé, se stesso *pron.* oneself
secchio *n.m.* bucket
secco *adj.* dry, sharp
secolo *n.m.* century
secondo *n.m., adj.* second
sedano *n.m.* celery
sedere *v.* to sit
sedia *n.f.* chair
segale *n.f.* rye
segnale *n.m.* sign
segnale stradale *n.m.* road sign
segreto *n.m.* secret
seguire *v.* to follow
selvatico *adj.* wild
semaforo *n.m.* traffic lights *pl.*
sembrare *v.* to seem

semplice *adj.* easy, simple
semplicemente *adv.* simply
sempre *adv.* always
senso *n.m.* sense
sentiero *n.m.* path
sentimento *n.m.* feeling
sentire *v.* to hear
sentirsi *v.ref.* to feel
senza *prep., conj.* without
separare *v.* to separate
separazione *n.f.* separation
sera *n.f.* evening
serio *adj.* serious
serpente *n.m.* snake
serrare *v.* to lock
serratura *n.f.* lock
servire *v.* to serve
servizio *n.m.* service
sessione *n.f.* session
sesso *n.m.* sex
seta *n.f.* silk
sete *n.f.* thirst
setta *n.f.* sect
settembre *n.m.* September
settentrionale *adj.* northern
settimana *n.f.* week
settore *n.m.* sector, field
sfiducia *n.f.* mistrust
sfortuna *n.f.* misfortune
sfortunatamente *adv.* unfortunately
sforzo *n.m.* effort
sgombro *n.m.* mackerel
sguardo *n.m.* look
sì *adv.* yes
sicuramente *adv.* surely
sicurezza *n.f.* safety; certainty
sigaretta *n.f.* cigarette
sigaro *n.m.* cigar
significare *v.* to mean

significato *n.m.* meaning
signora *n.f.* lady, Mrs.
signore *n.m.* gentleman, Mr., mister
signorina *n.f.* Miss
silenzio *n.m.* silence
simile *adj.* like, similar
sincerità *n.f.* sincerity
sincero *adj.* sincere
sinfonia *n.f.* symphony
singhiozzo *n.m.* hiccups *pl.*
sintetico *adj.* synthetic
sionista *n.m., adj.* Zionist
sistema *n.f.* system
situazione *n.f.* situation
sobborgo *n.m.* suburb
sobrio *adj.* sober
soccorrere *v.* to rescue
società *n.f.* society
soddisfare *v.* to satisfy
soddisfatto *adj.* satisfied
soffitto *n.m.* ceiling
soffrire *v.* to suffer
soggetto *n.m.* subject
sognare *v.* to dream
sogno *n.m.* dream
sole *n.m.* sun
solitario *adj.* lonely
solito *adj.* usual
solitudine *n.f.* solitude
sollevare *v.* to lift, to raise
sollievo *n.m.* relief
solo *adj., adv.* alone
sopra *prep.* on, upon, above
sopracciglia *(pl.) n.m.* eyebrows
soprannome *n.m.* nickname
sordità *n.f.* deafness
sorella *n.f.* sister
sorprendere *v.* to surprise
sorpresa *n.f.* surprise

sorridere *v.* to smile
sorriso *n.m.* smile
sorte *n.f.* lot, fate
sospettoso *adj.* suspicious
sospirare *v.* to sigh
sospiro *n.m.* sigh
sostegno *n.m.* support
sostenere *v.* to support
sotto *prep.* under
sottolineare *v.* to stress, to underline
Spagna *n.f.* Spain
spagnolo *n.m., adj.* Spanish
spalla *n.f.* shoulder
sparare *v.* to shoot
spazzola *n.f.* brush, hairbrush
spazzolare *v.* to brush
specchio *n.m.* mirror
speciale *adj.* special
specialmente *adv.* especially
specie *n.f.* species, kind, sort
spedire *v.* to send
spendere *v.* to spend
speranza *n.f.* hope
sperare *v.* to hope
spesa *n.f.* shopping, expense
spesso *adv.* often
spettacolo *n.m.* show
spezia *n.f.* spice
spia *n.f.* spy
spiacevole *adj.* unpleasant
spiaggia *n.f.* beach
spiegare *v.* to explain
spillo *n.f.* pin
spinaci *(pl.) n.m.* spinach *s.*
spingere *v.* to push
spirito *n.m.* spirit
spirituale *adj.* spiritual
splendore *n.m.* splendor
spogliarsi *v.ref.* to undress

sporcizia *n.f.* dirt
sporco *adj.* dirty
sposa *n.f.* bride
sposare *v.* to marry: *sposarsi (v.ref.)* to get married
sposato *adj.* married
sposo *n.m.* bridegroom
spostare *v.* to dislocate
sprecare *v.* to waste
spreco *n.m.* waste
spremuta *n.f.* juice
squalo *n.m.* shark
stagionale *adj.* seasonal
stagione *n.f.* season
stanotte *adv.* tonight
stanza *n.f.* room
starnutire *v.* to sneeze
Stati Uniti *(pl.) n.m.* United States
stato *n.m.* state
statua *n.f.* statue
statuto *n.m.* statute
stazione *n.f.* station
stella *n.f.* star
sterminare *v.* to exterminate
sterminio *n.m.* extermination
stesso *adj., pron.* same
stimare *v.* to estimate
stirare *v.* to iron
stivale *n.m.* boot
stomaco *n.m.* stomach
storia *n.f.* history, story
storico *adj.* historical
straccio *n.m.* rag
strada *n.f.* road, street
straniero *n.m.* stranger; *adj.* foreign
strano *adj.* strange
stretto *adj.* narrow, tight
strofa *n.f.* verse
strumento *n.m.* instrument; means

studente *n.m.* student
studiare *v.* to study
stufa *n.f.* stove
stufato *n.m.* stew
stupido *adj.* stupid
stuzzicadenti *n.m.* toothpick
subito *adv.* at once
successo *n.m.* success
Sud *n.m.* South
sudare *v.* to sweat
sudorazione *n.f.* perspiration
sudore *n.m.* sweat
sufficiente *adj.* enough
sugo *n.m.* sauce
suicidio *n.m.* suicide
suocera *n.f.* mother-in-law
suocero *n.m.* father-in-law
suonare *v.* to play (instrument); to ring (bell)
suora *n.f.* nun
superficie *n.f.* surface
supporre *v.* to suppose
suscettibile *adj.* sensitive
sussistenza *n.f.* livelihood
sussurrare *v.* to whisper
sussurro *n.m.* whisper
sveglia *n.f.* alarm clock
svegliarsi *v.ref.* to wake up
svenire *v.* to faint
sviluppo *n.m.* development
Svizzera *n.f.* Switzerland
svizzero *n.m., adj.* Swiss
svolta *n.f.* curve; turning

T

tabaccaio *n.m.* tobacconist
tacchino *n.m.* turkey
tagliare *v.* to cut
taglio *n.m.* cut

talento *n.m.* talent
tallone *n.m.* heel
tampone *n.m.* tampon
tappeto *n.m.* rug
tappo *n.m.* cork
tardi *adj., adv.* late
tariffa *n.f.* fare
tasca *n.f.* pocket
tassa *n.f.* tax
tasso *n.m.* rate
tavolino *n.m.* table
tazza *n.f.* cup, mug
tè *n.m.* tea
teatrale *adj.* theatrical
teatro *n.m.* theater
tedesco *n.m., adj.* German
tedioso *adj.* tedious
telefonare *v.* to call
telefonata *n.f.* telephone call
telefono *n.m.* telephone
telegramma *n.f.* telegram
televisione *n.f.* television
temere *v.* to be afraid
temperatura *n.f.* temperature
tempestivo *adj.* timely
tempo *n.m.* time
temporale *n.m.* storm
temporaneo *adj.* temporary
tenda *n.f.* blind; tent
tenere *v.* to hold, to keep
tenerezza *n.f.* tenderness
terminare *v.* to end
termometro *n.m.* thermometer
terra *n.f.* land
terrazza *n.f.* terrace
terribile *adj.* terrible
territorio *n.m.* territory
terrore *n.m.* terror
terzo *adj.* third

tessuto *n.m.* tissue
testa *n.f.* head
testamento *n.m.* testament, will
testimone *n.m.* witness
testimoniare *v.* to testify
tetano *n.m.* tetanus
tetro *adj.* gloomy
tetto *n.m.* roof
timido *adj.* shy
timo *n.m.* thyme
timpano *n.m.* drum
tintura *n.f.* dye
tipo *n.m.* type
tirare *v.* to pull
toccare *v.* to touch
tocco *n.m.* touch
tollerante *adj.* tolerant
tolleranza *n.f.* tolerance
tollerare *v.* to endure
tomba *n.f.* grave, tomb
tonno *n.m.* tuna
tonsille *(pl.)* *n.f.* tonsils
topo *n.m.* mouse
torre *n.f.* tower
torta *n.f.* cake
torto *n.m.* harm
tortura *n.f.* torture
torturare *v.* to torture
tosse *n.f.* cough
tossire *v.* to cough
totale *n.m.* amount, total
tovagliolo *n.m.* napkin
traccia *n.f.* track, trace
traditore *n.m.* traitor
tradizionale *adj.* traditional
tradizione *n.f.* tradition
tradurre *v.* to translate
traduttore *n.m.* translator
traduzione *n.f.* translation

traffico *n.m.* traffic
traguardo *n.m.* goal
tram *n.m.* trolley
tranne *prep.* except
tranquillante *n.m.* tranquilizer; *adj.* tranquilizing
tranquillo *adj.* peaceful, tranquil
trasalire *v.* to startle
trascorrere *v.* to spend time, to pass
trascurare *v.* to neglect
trascurato *adj.* neglected
trasferire *v.* to transfer
trasformatore *n.m.* adaptor
trasfusione *n.f.* blood transfusion
trasportare *v.* to transport
trasporto *n.m.* transportation
trattare *v.* to treat
tratto *n.m.* trait
tremendo *adj.* awful; tremendous
treno *n.m.* train
tribunale *n.m.* courthouse
triste *adj.* sad
tritare *v.* to mince
tromba *n.f.* trumpet
troppo *adv.* too
trota *n.f.* trout
trovare *v.* to find
trucco *n.m.* makeup
tu *pron.* you
tubo *n.m.* pipe
tuffarsi *v.ref.* to dive
tumore *n.m.* tumor
tuono *n.m.* thunder
tuorlo *n.m.* yolk
turchese *n.m.* turquoise
turco *adj.* Turkish
turista *n.f.* tourist
tutto *adj., pron.* all
tutto *pron.* everything

U

ubbidiente *adj.* obedient
ubbidienza *n.f.* obedience
ubriaco *adj.* drunk
uccello *n.m.* bird
uccidere *v.* to kill
ufficio *n.m.* office
ufficioso *adj.* unofficial
uguale *adj.* equal, same
ulcera *n.f.* ulcer
ulteriore *adv.* further
ultimo *adj.* last
umano *adj.* human
umidità *n.f.* humidity, damp
umido *adj.* damp, moist
umore *n.m.* mood
uncino *n.m.* hook
ungherese *n.m., adj.* Hungarian
Ungheria *n.f.* Hungary
unghia *n.f.* nail (finger)
unguento *n.m.* ointment
unirsi *v.ref.* to unite
università *n.f.* university
universo *n.m.* universe
unto *adj.* greasy
uomo *n.m.* man
uovo *n.m.* egg
uragano *n.m.* hurricane
urbano *adj.* urban
urgente *adj.* urgent
urina *n.f.* urine
urinare *v.* to urinate
urlare *v.* to scream, to yell
usanza *n.f.* custom
usare *v.* to use
usato *adj.* secondhand
usciere *n.m.* usher
uscire *v.* to exit, to go out

uscita *n.f.* exit
uso *n.m.* use
utensile *n.m.* utensil
utero *n.m.* uterus
utile *adj.* useful
uva *n.f.* grape
uvetta *n.f.* raisin

V

vacanza *n.f.* vacation
vaccinarsi *v.ref.* to vaccinate
vagabondare *v.* to wander
vaginale *adj.* vaginal
vago *adj.* vague
vagone *n.m.* wagon
valido *adj.* valid
valigia *n.f.* suitcase
valle *n.f.* valley
valore *n.m.* value
vandalismo *n.m.* vandalism
vandalo *n.m.* vandal
vano *adj.* vain
vantaggio *n.m.* advantage
vapore *n.m.* steam
varietà *n.f.* variety
vaso *n.m.* vase
vecchio *adj.* old
vedere *v.* to see
vedova *n.f.* widow
vedovo *n.m.* widower
veglia *n.f.* wake
veicolo *n.m.* vehicle
veleno *n.m.* poison
velenoso *adj.* poisonous
velo *n.m.* veil
velocità *n.f.* speed
vena *n.f.* vein

vendere *v.* to sell
vendetta *n.f.* revenge
venerdì *n.m.* Friday
venire *v.* to come
ventilatore *n.m.* fan
vento *n.m.* wind
verbo *n.m.* verb
verde *adj.* green
verdura *n.f.* vegetable
vergogna *n.f.* shame
verità *n.f.* truth
vero *adj.* true
versare *v.* to pour
versione *n.f.* version
verso *prep.* toward(s)
vestiti *(pl.)* *n.m.* clothes
vestito *n.m.* dress
veterinario *n.m.* veterinary
vetro *n.m.* glass
vettura *n.f.* carriage, coach
via *adv.* away
via *n.f.* way, street
viaggiare *v.* to travel
viaggiatore *n.m.* traveller
viaggio *n.m.* journey, voyage
vicinato *n.m.* neighborhood
vicino *adj., prep.* near
vicino *n.m.* neighbor
vicino (a) *prep.* close (to)
vicolo *n.m.* alley
vigna *n.f.* vineyard
vile *adj.* vile
villaggio *n.m.* village
vincere *v.* to win
vino *n.m.* wine
violento *adj.* violent
violenza *n.f.* violence
violino *n.m.* violin

virtù *n.f.* virtue
visibile *adj.* visible
visione *n.f.* sight, vision
visita *n.f.* visit
visitare *v.* to visit
vista *n.f.* view
visto *n.m.* visa
vita *n.f.* life
vitamina *n.f.* vitamin
vitello *n.m.* veal
vittima *n.f.* victim
vittoria *n.f.* victory
vivere *v.* to live
vivo *adj.* alive
viziare *v.* to spoil
viziato *adj.* spoilt
vocabolario *n.m.* vocabulary
vocale *n.f.* vowel
voce *n.f.* voice
volare *v.* to fly
volere *v.* to want
volgare *adj.* vulgar
volontà *n.f.* will
volontario *n.m., adj.* volunteer
volta *n.f.* time *(occasion)*; vault
voltaggio *n.m.* voltage
voltarsi *v.ref.* to turn (around, over, to)
volto *n.m.* face
vomitare *v.* to vomit
vongola *n.f.* clam
votare *v.* to vote
voto *n.m.* vote
vuoto *adj.* empty, vacant

X

xenofobia *n.f.* xenophobia

Z

zafferano *n.m.* saffron
zanzara *n.f.* mosquito
zebra *n.f.* zebra
zelo *n.m.* zeal
zero *n.m.* zero
zia *n.f.* aunt
zinco *n.m.* zinc
zingaro *n.m.* gypsy
zio *n.m.* uncle
zolletta *n.f.* lump
zona *n.f.* zone
zoo *n.m.* zoo
zoologia *n.f.* zoology
zoologico *adj.* zoological
zucca *n.f.* pumpkin
zucchero *n.m.* sugar

ENGLISH-ITALIAN DICTIONARY
*Verbs are indicated by (to).

A

abbey abbazia
abbreviation abbreviazione
abdomen addome
abhor (to) aborrire
able (to be able to) potere, essere capace
about circa, riguardo a
above sopra, al di sopra
absent assente
absurd assurdo
abuse (to) abusare
accept (to) accettare
accessories *(pl.)* accessorio *s.*
accident incidente
accommodation alloggio
account acconto
accusation accusa
accuse (to) accusare
ache dolore
ache (to) dolere, far male
acquaintance conoscenza
act atto
action azione
activity attività
actor attore
actress attrice
actually veramente, in realtà, infatti
adaptor trasformatore (di corrente)
add (to) aggiungere
address indirizzo
admire (to) ammirare
admission ammissione, entrata
adult adulto
advantage vantaggio

adventure avventura
advertisement pubblicità, locandina
advice consiglio
advise (to) consigliare
afraid (to be afraid) aver paura, temere
Africa Africa
after dopo, poi, successivamente
afternoon pomeriggio
again nuovamente, di nuovo, ancora
against contro, contrario
age età
ago fa
agree (to) essere d'accordo, accordarsi, accettare
agreeable piacevole, gradevole
agreement accordo, patto
aimless senza scopo
air aria
air-conditioning aria condizionata
airmail posta aerea
airplane aeroplano
airport aeroporto
airsickness mal d'aria
alabaster alabastro
alarm clock sveglia
alcohol alcol
alive vivo, in vita
all *adj., pron.* tutto, tutti
allergic allergico
allergy allergia
alley vicolo
allow (to) permettere
allowed permesso, concesso
almond mandorla
almost quasi
alone solo
alphabet alfabeto
already già
also anche, inoltre
although malgrado, benché

always sempre
amazing sorprendente, stupefacente
ambitious ambizioso
ambulance ambulanza
America America
American americano
amount ammontare, somma, totale
anchovy alice, acciuga
and e
anesthetic anestetico
angel angelo
anger ira, rabbia
angry irato, arrabbiato, adirato
angry (to be) adirarsi, arrabbiarsi
animal animale
ankle caviglia
anniversary anniversario
announce (to) annunciare
annoy (to) infastidire, irritare
annoyed infastidito, irritato
another un altro, un'altra
answer (to) rispondere
answer risposta
ant formica
anthem inno
antibiotic antibiotico
antidepressant antidepressivo
antiques *(pl.)* antiquariato *s.*
antique shop antiquario
antiseptic antisettico
anyone chiunque; nessuno
anything qualunque cosa, qualsiasi cosa; niente
apartment appartamento
aperitif aperitivo
appear (to) apparire, sembrare, comparire
appendicitis appendicite
appetizer aperitivo, assaggino, antipasto
apple mela
appointment appuntamento

apricot albicocca
April aprile
archaeology archeologia
architect architetto
arid arido
arm braccio
around intorno, in giro; circa
arrest (to) arrestare
arrival arrivo
arrive (to) arrivare
art arte
artery arteria
artichoke carciofo
artificial artificiale
artist artista
as come, (tanto) quanto
ashamed imbarazzato, vergognoso
ashtray posacenere
Asia Asia
ask for (to) chiedere, domandare
asparagus asparago
aspirin aspirina
associate (to) associare
assortment assortimento
assure (to) assicurare, assicurarsi
asthma asma
at a
at least almeno
at once immediatamente, subito
attack attacco
attractive attraente
audience pubblico
August agosto
aunt zia
Austria Austria
automatic automatico
autumn autunno
average *adj.* medio, normale

away via, lontano
awful orrendo, tremendo, terribile

B

baby bimbo
babysitter bambinaia
back *adj.* indietro; *prep.* dietro; *n.* schiena
backache mal di schiena
bacon pancetta, lardo affumicato
bad cattivo, male
bag borsa, sacco, bagaglio
bake (to) cuocere al forno
baker fornaio
balance bilancio, equilibrio
balcony balcone, balconata
bald calvo
ball palla, pallone
ballet balletto
banana banana
bandage bende, fasciatura
band-aid cerotto
bank banca
baptism battesimo
bar pub, locale notturno
barbecue barbecue, brace, alla brace
barber barbiere
barely appena, apertamente
bark (to) abbaiare, latrare
barrel barile
basil basilico
basin bacino, catino, lavabo
basket cesto
bath bagno
bathe (to) farsi il bagno
bathing suit costume da bagno
bathroom stanza da bagno, bagno, toilette
bathtub vasca da bagno

battery batteria
bay bai; alloro (*bot.*)
be (to) essere
beach spiaggia
bean fagiolo
beard barba
beautiful bello, bellissimo
beauty bellezza, beltà
because perché, poiché
become (to) diventare, divenire
bed letto
bee ape
beef manzo
beer birra
before prima
beggar mendicante
begin (to) iniziare, cominciare
beginner principiante
beginning inizio, principio
behind *prep.* dietro, di dietro, indietro
being esistenza, l'essere
believe (to) credere
bell campana, campanello
below sotto, al di sotto, giù
belt cintura, cinta
bench panchina
bend curva
best (the) il migliore
between fra, tra, in mezzo a
beware! Attenzione!
bicycle bicicletta
big grande
bill conto, fattura
binoculars (*pl.*) binocolo *s.*
biography biografia
bird uccello
birth nascita
birthday compleanno
biscuit biscotto

bit pezzettino, un poco
bitter amaro
black nero
black and white bianco e nero
blackboard lavagna
blanket coperta
bleed (to) sanguinare
bless (to) benedire
blind *adj.* cieco
blind (window) persiana, tenda
blister bolla
block isolato
block (to) bloccare
blood sangue
blood pressure pressione del sangue
blood transfusion trasfusione (di sangue)
blouse camicetta
blue blu, azzurro, celeste
boat barca
boil (to) bollire
boiled bollito, lesso
bone osso
book libro
bookstore libreria
boot stivale, scarpa
boring noioso, tedioso
born nato
botanical botanico
both entrambi, tutti e due
bottle bottiglia
bottle opener apribottiglie
bottom fondo
bowels *(pl.)* viscere
box scatola
boy ragazzo, ragazzino
bra reggiseno, reggipetto
bracelet braccialetto
brain cervello
brake freno

branch ramo, succursale, filiale
brave *adj.* coraggioso
bread pane
break (to) rompere, spezzare
breakdown collasso, rottura, esaurimento
breakfast colazione
breast petto, sterno, seno
breath respiro
breathe (to) respirare
breeze brezza, venticello
bride sposa
bridegroom sposo
bridge ponte
brief breve, riassunto
bring (to) portare
broad ampio, largo
broken rotto
bronze bronzo
broom scopa, ramazza
brother fratello
brother-in-law cognato
brown marrone
bruise livido
brush spazzola *(hair)*; spazzolino *(tooth)*; pennello *(paint)*
brush (to) spazzolare
bucket secchio
build (to) costruire
building costruzione, edificio
bulb bulbo, lampadina
bull toro
burn (to) bruciare
bus autobus
business impresa, affare
bus station capolinea (dell'autobus)
bus stop fermata dell'auto
busy occupato, impegnato, preso
but ma
butcher macellaio
butter burro

butterfly farfalla
button bottone
buy (to) comprare, acquistare

C

cabbage cavolo
cabin capanna, cabina
cable cavo, cablogramma
café bar, caffè bar
caffeine caffeina
caffeine-free decaffeinato
cake dolce, torta
calculator calcolatrice
calendar calendario, almanacco
call (telephone) telefonata
call (to) chiamare, telefonare
calm *n.* calma; *adj.* calmo
camera macchinetta fotografica
camp (to) fare campeggio, campeggiare
can *n.* scatoletta, bidone
can (to be able to) potere
cancel (to) cancellare, disdire
cancer cancro
candle candela
cap berretto
capable capace, abile
caper cappero
capital capitale; capitello *(arch.)*
car macchina
card carta, scheda, biglietto
care cura, attenzione
careful attento, premuroso
caress carezza
carp carpa
carrot carota
carry (to) portare, trasportare
cash contante, liquidi

cashier cassiere, cassa
cassette cassetta
castle castello
cat gatto
catacomb catacomba
catalog catalogo
cathedral cattedrale
catholic cattolico
cauliflower cavolfiore
caution cautela
cave caverna, grotta
ceiling soffitto
celery sedano
cemetery cimitero
center centro
centimeter centimetro
century secolo
ceramic ceramica
cereal cereali, grano
certificate certificato
chain catena
chair sedia
chance occasione, avvenimento fortuito
change cambiamento; resto (*money*)
change (to) cambiare, permutare
chapel cappella
charge prezzo, spesa; accusa
cheap a buon mercato
check controllo, scontrino; assegno
check (to) controllare, verificare
checkbook libretto degli assegni
check-in accettazione, check-in
cheers! Alla salute! Cin cin!
cheese formaggio
chef chef, cuoco
cherry ciliegia, ciliegina
chess scacchi *pl.*
chestnut castagna
chicken pollo

chickpea cecio (*pl.* ceci)
chicory cicoria
child bambino
Chinese cinese
chocolate cioccolato, cioccolata
choice scelta
choose (to) scegliere
Christmas Natale
church chiesa
cigar sigaro
cigarette sigaretta
cinema cinema
cinnamon cannella
circle circolo, giro
citizen cittadino, abitante
city città
clam vongola
class classe
clean pulito
clean (to) pulire
clear chiaro
clerk impiegato
clever intelligente
cliff scogliera, rocce
climate clima, temperatura
clock orologio
close vicino
close (to) chiudere
closed chiuso
clothes *(pl.)* abiti, vestiti
cloud nuvola
coat cappotto, giacca
cockroach scarafaggio, bacarozzo
cod merluzzo
coffee caffè
coin moneta
cold *adj.* freddo
cold raffreddore (*illness*)
colleague collega

color *n.* colore
come (to) venire
comedy commedia
commission commissione
common comune
compartment compartimento
compass bussola
complaint lamentela, reclamo
composer compositore
concentrate (to) concentrarsi
concert concerto
condom preservativo
conductor direttore (*mus.*); capotreno; conducente
confidence fiducia, confidenza
confirm (to) confermare
congratulations *(pl.)* congratulazioni, auguri
congress congresso
consequence conseguenza
constipated costipato
constitution costituzione
contact contatto
contact lens lenti a contatto
contain (to) contenere
contemporary contemporaneo
contraceptive contraccettivo, preservativo
contract contratto
control controllo
convent convento
convert (to) convertire, convertirsi
cook cuoco
cook (to) cucinare
copper rame
cork tappo
corkscrew cavatappi, cavaturaccioli
corner angolo
cosmic cosmico
cost costo
cost (to) costare
cotton cotone
cough tosse

cough (to) tossire
countryside campagna
courthouse corte, tribunale
cousin cugino, cugina
crab granchio
cramp crampo
cream crema, panna
credit credito, accredito
credit card carta di credito
criminal criminale
crisis crisi
cross croce
cross (to) attraversare
crossing incrocio, strisce pedonali
crutches *(pl.)* grucce
cry (to) piangere
crystal cristallo
cucumber cetriolo
cup tazza, coppa
currency moneta, corso monetario
current corrente
curtain tenda, cortina
curve curva, svolta
custom costume, uso
customer cliente
customs *(pl.)* dogana *s.*
cut (to) tagliare
cut (wound) taglio, ferita
cylinder cilindro

D

dad papà, padre
damage danno
damp *n.* umidità; *adj.* umido
dance (to) ballare, danzare
danger pericolo
dangerous pericoloso

dare (to) osare
daring coraggioso, audace
dark *adj.* buio, scuro
darkness oscurità
darling caro
date data; dattero (*fruit*)
daughter figlia
daughter-in-law nuora
day giorno
daybreak alba
dead morto, deceduto
deadline scadenza
deaf sordo
dear caro
death morte
debt debito
decaffeinated decaffeinato
December dicembre
decide (to) decidere
decision decisione
decoration decorazione
deep *adj.* profondo
defective difettoso, difettivo
defend (to) difendere
delay ritardo
delicate delicato
delicious delizioso
deliver (to) consegnare
demand richiesta, esigenza
demand (to) esigere, richiedere
demolish (to) demolire
dense denso, opaco
dentist dentista
deodorant deodorante
depart (to) partire, allontanarsi
department reparto, dipartimento
departure partenza
depend (to) dipendere (da)

deposit deposito
describe (to) descrivere
desperate disperato
despite malgrado
destiny destino
destroy (to) distruggere
detour deviazione
develop (to) sviluppare
development sviluppo
devote (to) dedicare
diabetes diabete
diabetic diabetico
diamond diamante
diarrhea diarrea
diary diario
dictionary dizionario
die (to) morire, perire
diet dieta
dietetic dietetico
difference differenza, diversità
difficult difficile, arduo
difficulty difficoltà
digest (to) digerire
digital digitale
diligent diligente
dine (to) cenare
dining room sala da pranzo
dinner cena
direct diretto
direction direzione
director direttore
dirt sporcizia, sporco
dirty sporco
disabled inabile, disabile
disappear (to) scomparire
disappointed deluso
discover (to) scoprire
disease malattia
disgusting disgustoso

dish piatto
dishonest disonesto
disk disco, dischetto
dislike avversione
dislocate (to) dislocare, spostare
disobedience disobbedienza
dissatisfied insoddisfatto
distance distanza, lontananza
district distretto
disturb (to) disturbare
disturbance agitazione
dive (to) tuffarsi
divorce divorzio
divorce (to) divorziare
divorced *adj.* divorziato
dizzy stordito
do (to) fare
doctor dottore
document documento
dog cane
doll bambola
dollar dollaro
donkey asino, asinello
door porta
dormitory dormitorio
double doppio
doubt (to) dubitare
dough pasta, impasto
doughnut ciambella pasticcera
down *adv., prep.* giù, di sotto
downstairs dabbasso
downtown centro città
dozen dozzina
draft corrente d'aria, abbozzo
drawer cassetto
dream sogno
dream (to) sognare
dress vestito, abito
drink bibita

drink (to) bere
drive (to) guidare
driving licence patente
drop goccia
drug droga, medicina
drum tamburo, timpano
drunk *adj.* ubriaco
dry secco, asciutto
dry (to) asciugare, essiccare
dry cleaner lavanderia
duck anatra
dull sciocco, triste, noioso
during durante
dusk crepuscolo, oscurità
dust polvere
duty dovere, ubbidienza
dye tinta, tintura

E

each ogni, ciascuno
eagle aquila
ear orecchio
early presto, primo, prematuro
earn (to) guadagnare
East Est
Easter Pasqua
Eastern orientale
easy semplice, facile
eat (to) mangiare
edge orlo, margine
education istruzione
effort sforzo
egg uovo (*pl.* uova)
eggplant melanzana
egoist egoista
eight otto
eighteen diciotto

eighty ottanta
either l'uno o l'altro, entrambi
elect (to) eleggere
election elezione
electric elettrico
electricity elettricità
electronic elettronico
elephant elefante
elevator ascensore
eleven undici
elsewhere altrove
embarrassment imbarazzo
embrace abbraccio, amplesso
embrace (to) abbracciare
emergency emergenza
emigration emigrazione
empty vuoto
end fine
end (to) finire, terminare
endure (to) sopportare, tollerare
enemy nemico
energetic energetico
engaged impegnato; fidanzato
engagement impegno; fidanzamento
engine motore, macchinario
engineer ingegnere
England Inghilterra, Gran Bretagna
English inglese, britannico
enjoy (to enjoy oneself) divertirsi, intrattenersi
enjoyable divertente, gradevole
enlarge (to) allargare
enough abbastanza, sufficientemente
enrage (to) esasperare, far arrabbiare
ensure (to) assicurare, garantire
enter (to) entrare
entertain (to) intrattenere
enthusiastic entusiasta
entrance ingresso, entrata
entry entrata, passaggio

envelope busta (da lettere)
envy invidia
envy (to) invidiare
epileptic epilettico
equally ugualmente
equipment equipaggiamento, attrezzatura
eraser gomma per cancellare
escape fuga, evasione
especially specialmente
esteemed stimato
eternity eternità
Europe Europa
European europeo
even *adj.* paro; *adv.* persino
evening sera
every ogni, ciascuno, tutti
everything tutto, ogni cosa
everywhere in ogni dove, ovunque
evidently evidentemente
examination esame, ispezione
example esempio
excellent eccellente
except eccetto, tranne
exception eccezione
exceptional eccezionale
exchange cambio (moneta)
exchange (to) scambiare
excited eccitato
excursion escursione
excuse scusa, giustificazione
excuse (to) scusare, giustificare
exercise esercizio
exercise (to) esercitare, esercitarsi
exhausted esausto
exile esilio
exit uscita
expect (to) aspettare, aspettarsi; esigere
expenses spese
expensive costoso, caro

experience esperienza
expert *n.* esperto
explain (to) spiegare
express espresso
express (to) esprimere
extensive esteso, completo, ampio
extent estensione, grado
exterminate (to) sterminare
extinguish (to) spegnere, estinguere
extract estratto, citazione
extreme estremo
eye occhio
eyebrow sopracciglia *pl.*
eye drops *(pl.)* gocce per gli occhi
eyeglasses *(pl.)* occhiali
eyesight vista

F

face faccia, volto
factory industria
failure fallimento, guasto
faint (to) svenire
faith fede
falcon falcone
fall caduta, cascata; autunno
fall (to) cadere
false falso
family famiglia
famous famoso
fan ventilatore, ventaglio
fanatic fanatico
fantastic fantastico
far lontano
fare tariffa
farm fattoria
farmer fattore, contadino
fashion moda, stile

fat grasso
father padre, papà
father-in-law suocero
fault colpa
favor *n.* favore, piacere
favorite preferito
fear *n.* paura, timore
feast festa, banchetto
February febbraio
fee tassa, tariffa, onorario
feel (to) sentire, sentirsi, provare
feeling sentimento
fellow compagno, individuo
feminine femminile
fence recinto
fermentation fermentazione
festival festival
festivity festività, celebrazione
fever febbre
few pochi
fiancé fidanzato
fiancée fidanzata
fidelity fedeltà
field campo
fifteen quindici
fifth quinto
fifty cinquanta
fig fico
fight combattimento, lotta
figure figura, forma
file lima; schedario, archivio
fill (to) riempire
fillet filetto
filling ripieno
film pellicola
filter filtro
finally alla fine, finalmente
financial finanziario
find (to) trovare

fine fine, bello
finger dito (*pl.* dita)
finish (to) finire
fire fuoco
fireworks *(pl.)* fuochi d'artificio
firm ditta
first primo
fish pesce
fit adatto
five cinque
fix (to) riparare, fissare
flag bandiera
flannel flanella
flatter (to) lusingare, adulare
flaw falla, crepa
flea market mercatino delle pulci
flexible flessibile
floor pavimento
florist fioraio
flour farina
flow (to) scorrere, fluire
flower fiore
flu raffreddore
fly mosca
fly (to) volare
fog nebbia
foggy nebbioso
follow (to) seguire
food cibo
fool sciocco, buffone
foot piede
for per
forbid (to) proibire, impedire
forbidden proibito
force forza
force (to) forzare
forehead fronte
foreign *adj.* straniero
foreigner *n.* straniero

forest foresta
forget (to) dimenticare, scordare
forgive (to) perdonare
fork forchetta
form forma
fortnight due settimane *pl.*, quindici giorni *pl.*
fortress fortezza
fortunately fortunatamente
forward avanti
foundation fondazione
fountain fontana
fracture frattura
fragile fragile
France Francia
Franciscan francescano
free libero; gratis
freedom libertà
freight trasporto, nolo
French francese
fresh fresco
Friday venerdì
fridge frigorifero
fried fritto
friend amico
friendly amichevole
frivolous frivolo
frog rana
from da
front anteriore, frontale, fronte
frost gelo, brina
frozen gelato, surgelato
fruit frutta
fry (to) friggere
fuel gas, carburante
full pieno
fun divertimento
function (to) funzionare, operare
funeral funerale
funny divertente

fur pelliccia
furious furioso, arrabbiato
furniture mobilio
further ulteriore, oltre, più lontano
fuse valvola, fusibile
future futuro

G

game giuoco
garage garage
garbage immondizia, rifiuti *pl.*
garden giardino
garlic aglio
gas gas
gasoline benzina
gastritis gastrite
gate portone, cancello, cancellata
gather (to) riunire, riunirsi
gathering riunione *(meeting)*; raccolta
gay gaio, gioioso; omosessuale
gear meccanismo, marcia, cambio
general generale
generally generalmente
generosity generosità
genitals genitali
gentleman gentiluomo
genuine genuino
German tedesco
Germany Germania
get (to) ottenere, prendere, arrivare *(movement)*
gift regalo
girl ragazza
give (to) dare, regalare
glad contento, felice
gland ghiandola
glass vetro, di vetro; bicchiere
glaze superficie vetrosa

globe globo
gloomy tetro, cupo
glove guanto
glue colla
go (to) andare, recarsi
goal scopo, fine, traguardo
goat capra
god dio
gold oro
golden d'oro
good buono
Good-bye! Addio!
goods *(pl.)* beni, merce *s.*
goose oca
gossip pettegolezzo, voce
government governo
grain grano, chicco
gram grammo
granddaughter nipote *(f.)*
grandfather nonno
grandmother nonna
grandson nipote *(m.)*
grape acino; uva
grapefruit pompelmo
grass erba
grave *n.* tomba; *adj.* grave, serio
gravy sugo
grease grasso
great grande, magnifico
Greece Grecia
Greek greco
green verde
greengrocer erbivendolo, fruttivendolo
greetings *(pl.)* saluti, auguri
gray grigio
grief *n.* dolore, cordoglio
group gruppo
grow (to) crescere
guarantee garanzia

guest ospite
guesthouse pensione
guide guida
guidebook guida
guitar chitarra
gum gomma, gengiva
gun arma da fuoco, fucile, pistola
gymnastics *(pl.)* ginnastica *s.*
gynecologist ginecologo
gypsy zingaro

H

habit abitudine, usanza
hair capello
hairbrush spazzola
hairdresser parrucchiere
hairdryer asciugacapelli
half metà
hall sala, salone, refettorio
ham prosciutto
hammer martello
hand mano
handbag bagaglio a mano, borsetta
handkerchief fazzoletto
handle maniglia, manico, impugnatura
handmade manifattura, fatto a mano
handsome bello, di bell'aspetto
hang (to) appendere, impiccare
hanger stampella, attaccapanni
happen (to) succedere, accadere
happiness felicità
happy felice
harbor porto, rifugio
hard duro, difficile
hardly appena, a stento
harm danno, torto
harvest raccolto, messe

harvest (to) mietere
hat cappello
hate (to) odiare
hatred odio
have (to) avere
hazelnut nocciola
he egli, lui
head testa, capo
headache mal di testa
headlight faro
health salute
healthy in salute, salutare
hear (to) sentire
heart cuore
heat calore, calura
heaven paradiso, cielo
heavy pesante
heel tallone, calcagno
height altezza
helicopter elicottero
hell inferno
Hello! Salve!
help aiuto
help (to) aiutare
herbs *(pl.)* erbe
here qui, qua
heritage eredità
herring aringa
Hi! Ciao!
hiccups *(pl.)* singhiozzo *s.*
hidden nascosto
hide (to) nascondere
high alto, elevato
hill collina
hillside pendio
hire (to) assumere
historical storico
history storia
hit (to) colpire

hitchhike (to) fare l'autostop
hold (to) abbracciare, tenere, contenere
hole buco
holiday festa, festività
home casa
honest onesto
honey miele
honeymoon luna di miele
honor onore
hook gancio, uncino
hope speranza
hope (to) sperare
horror orrore
hors d'oeuvre antipasto
horse cavallo
hospital ospedale
hostage ostaggio
hot bollente, caldo
hotel hotel
hot-water bottle borsa dell'acqua calda
hour ora
house casa
household famiglia, membri della famiglia *pl.*
housekeeper governante, domestica
housewife massaia, casalinga
how come
however comunque, tuttavia, però
huge enorme, grandissimo
human umano
hundred cento
Hungarian ungherese
Hungary Ungheria
hunger fame, appetito
hungry affamato
hunter cacciatore
hurricane uragano
hurry (in a) frettoloso, di fretta
hurry (to) affrettarsi, sbrigarsi
hurt (to be) essere ferito

hurt (to) ferire
husband marito

I

I io
ice ghiaccio
ice cream gelato
idea idea
identity identità
idiot idiota
if se
ignition accensione
ill malato, ammalato
illegitimate illegittimo
illness malattia
image immagine
imagine (to) immaginare
immediately immediatamente
immoral immorale
immortal immortale
immunization immunizzazione
impatient impaziente
impersonal impersonale
important importante
impossible impossibile
impression impressione
impressive impressionante
improper inappropriato, inadatto
improve (to) migliorare, perfezionare
in in
incapable incapace
incident incidente
include (to) includere
incomprehensible incomprensibile
increase incremento, aumento
increase (to) incrementare, aumentare
incredible incredibile

indeed davvero, in verità
independence indipendenza
independent indipendente
indigestion indigestione
industry industria
inexpensive a poco prezzo, poco costoso
infection infezione
inflammable infiammabile
inflammation infiammazione
influenza influenza
information informazione
infraction infrazione
ingratitude ingratitudine
inherit (to) ereditare
inheritance eredità
injection iniezione
injured ferito
injury ferita, torto, danno
ink inchiostro
innocent innocente
inquire (to) indagare
insane pazzo
insect insetto
inside dentro
instead (of) invece di, piuttosto che
institute istituto
instrument strumento
insult insulto
insult (to) insultare
insurance assicurazione
interest interesse
interest (to) interessare, interessarsi
interested (in) interessato (a)
interesting interessante
intermission intermezzo, pausa
international internazionale
interpreter interprete
interrogation interrogatorio
intersection incrocio

intestines *(pl.)* intestino *s.*
introduce (to) presentare
introduction presentazione
invalid invalido
invest (to) investire
investigate (to) investigare
investigation investigazione
investment investimento
invitation invito
invite (to) invitare
invoice fattura
iodine iodio
Ireland Irlanda
Irish irlandese
iron ferro, ferro da stiro
iron (to) stirare
irregular irregolare
irresponsible irresponsabile
irritate (to) irritare
island isola
Israel Israele
Israeli israeliano
Italian italiano
Italy Italia
itch (to) prudere
ivory avorio

J

jacket giacca, giacchetta
jail prigione
jam marmellata
January gennaio
Japan Giappone
Japanese giapponese
jaw mascella, mandibola
jealous geloso
jealousy gelosia

jelly gelatina
Jew ebreo
jewel gioiello
jewelry gioielleria
Jewish ebraico
joint giuntura, articolazione
joke battuta, scherzo
joke (to) scherzare
journey viaggio
judge giudice
judge (to) giudicare
judgment giudizio
jug caraffa, boccale
juice succo, spremuta
July luglio
jump (to) saltare
June giugno
just giusto
just (only) solo, solamente, appena
justice giustizia

K

keep (to) tenere, mantenere
kerchief fazzoletto
kettle bollitore, bricco
key chiave
kidney rene
kill (to) uccidere, assassinare
kilogram chilogrammo, chilo
kilometer chilometro
kind *adj.* gentile, cortese; *n.* specie, tipo
kindly cortesemente
kindness gentilezza, cortesia
king re
kiosk chiosco
kiss bacio
kiss (to) baciare

kitchen cucina
knee ginocchio (*pl. ginocchia*)
kneel (to) inginocchiarsi
knife coltello
knock (to) bussare
know (to) sapere, conoscere

L

label etichetta
label (to) etichettare
lace laccio, pizzo
lack mancanza
lack (to) mancare, scarseggiare
lad giovanotto
ladder scala a pioli
lady signora
lake lago
lamb agnello
lamp lampada
land terra, paese
landscape paesaggio
language lingua
lantern lanterna
lard lardo
large largo, ampio
last ultimo
last (to) durare
late (to be) essere in ritardo, far tardi
later più tardi
laugh (to) (at) ridere (di)
laundry lavanderia, bucato
law legge
lawyer avvocato, legale
laxative lassativo
lazy pigro
lead piombo
lead (to) condurre, guidare

leader capo, guida
leaf foglia
learn (to) imparare
leather pelle, cuoio
leave (to) lasciare, abbandonare
leftovers *(pl.)* avanzi
leg gamba
lemon limone
lemonade limonata
lend (to) imprestare, prestare
length durata, lunghezza
lens lente, foto obiettivo
lentil lenticchia
less meno
lesson lezione
let (to) lasciare, consentire
letter lettera
lettuce lattuga
liar bugiardo
liberation liberazione
library biblioteca
lie (to) mentire; giacere
life vita
lift (to) alzare, sollevare
light *n.* luce
light *adj.* leggero
light (to) illuminare, accendere
lightning fulmine, lampo
like *adv.* come; *adj.* simile (a)
like (to) piacere (v.int.), volere
line linea
linen di lino
lion leone
lip labbro *(pl. labbra)*
lipstick rossetto
liqueur liquore
liquid liquido
listen (to) ascoltare

literature letteratura
liter litro
litter sporcizia, rifiuti *pl.*; barella
little piccolo, poco
live (to) vivere
livelihood mezzi di sussistenza
liver fegato
lizard lucertola
lobster aragosta
local locale
locate (to) collocare
lock serratura
lock (to) serrare
locksmith ferramenta
lonely solitario, solo
long lungo
look sguardo
look (to) guardare
lose (to) perdere
loss perdita
lost perso, sperduto
lot sorte
lot (a lot of) molto, un sacco (di)
lotion lozione
lottery lotteria
loud forte, ad alto volume
love amore
love (to) amare
lovely amabile
lover amante
low basso, a voce bassa
luck fortuna
luggage bagaglio
lump mucchio, gonfiore, zolletta
lunch pranzo
lunch (to have) pranzare
lungs *(pl.)* polmoni
luxury lusso, lussuria

M

machine macchina
mackerel sgombro
mad matto (*crazy*)
madman matto, pazzo
magazine rivista
magnificent magnifico
maiden fanciulla, vergine
mail (to) imbucare, spedire
mailbox cassetta della posta
main principale, centrale
maintain (to) mantenere
majority maggioranza
make (to) fare, costruire
makeup trucco
man uomo
manager manager, capoufficio
manual manuale
many molti, parecchi
map cartina, mappa
March marzo
margarine margarina
marinated marinato
marjoram maggiorana
market mercato
marmalade conserva, marmellata
married sposato
marry (to) sposare, sposarsi
mass massa, ammasso; messa
match incontro (*sport*); fiammifero
material materiale
mathematics (*pl.*) matematica *s.*
mattress materasso
May maggio
maybe forse, può darsi
meal pasto
mean *adj.* meschino

mean (to) significare
meaning significato
means mezzi
meanwhile nel mentre, nel frattempo
measles morbillo
measure misura
measure (to) misurare
measurement misurazione, calcolo
meat carne
meatball polpetta
mechanic meccanico
medicine medicinale, medicina
Mediterranean *adj.* mediterraneo
meet (to) incontrare
meeting incontro
melon melone
member membro
memory memoria
menu menu, lista delle vivande
mercy pietà, grazia
merrily felicemente, allegramente
merry gaio
mess confusione
message messaggio
meter metro
middle medio, di mezzo, centrale
Middle Ages Medioevo
midnight mezzanotte
midwife levatrice
mileage chilometraggio
milk latte
million milione
mince carne tritata
mind mente
mine mio
mineral minerale
minor minore, minorenne
minute minuto
mirror specchio

miserable miserabile, triste
Miss Signorina
mistake errore, sbaglio
mistrust sfiducia
misunderstand (to) fraintendere
misunderstanding fraintendimento
mix (to) miscelare, mischiare
modern moderno
modesty modestia
moist umido
moisturizer idratante
moment momento
Monday lunedì
money denaro, soldi *pl.*
monk monaco
monkey scimmia
monster mostro
month mese
monument monumento
mood umore
moon luna
moral morale
more più
morning mattino, mattina
mosque moschea
mosquito zanzara
most (the) il più
mostly per lo più
mother madre
mother-in-law suocera
motion mozione, movimento
motorbike motorino, scooter
motorcycle motocicletta
mountain montagna
mournful lugubre
mouse topo
moustache baffi *pl.*
mouth bocca
move (to) muovere, spostare; cambiar casa

movies *pl.* film
Mr., mister Signor
Mrs. Signora
much molto
mud fango
mug tazza
multiplication moltiplicazione
murder assassinio
murderer assassino
muscle muscolo
museum museo
mushroom fungo
music musica
must *v.* dovere
mustard mostarda
mute muto
mutual mutuo
my mio
mystery mistero

N

nail unghia *(finger)*, chiodo
naked nudo
name nome
napkin tovagliolo
narrow stretto
nation nazione
national nazionale
native *n., adj.* nativo; *adj.* oriundo
nature natura
nausea nausea
near vicino, prossimo
nearly quasi
necessary necessario
necessity necessità
neck collo
necklace collana, girocollo

necktie cravatta
need bisogno
need (to) abbisognare
needle ago
negative negativo
neglect (to) trascurare
neglected trascurato
neighbor vicino di casa
neighborhood vicinato
neither nessuno dei due, né…né
nephew nipote *(m.)*
nerve nervo
nervous nervoso
neurotic nevrotico
never mai
new nuovo
New Year's Eve capodanno
news *(pl.)* notizie, notiziario *s.*
newspaper giornale, quotidiano
next prossimo
nice carino
nickname soprannome
niece nipote *(f.)*
night notte
nine nove
nineteen diciannove
ninety novanta
no no
nobody nessuno
noisy rumoroso
non-alcoholic analcolico
none nessuno
nonsense nonsenso, assurdità
normal normale
North Nord
northern nordico, settentrionale
nose naso
not non
notebook quaderno

nothing niente, nulla
notice avviso, avvertimento, nota
notice (to) notare, osservare
nourish (to) nutrire
nourishment nutrimento, alimento
novel romanzo
November novembre
now ora, adesso
nowhere da nessuna parte
number numero
nun suora
nurse infermiera
nut noce

O

oak quercia
obedient ubbidiente
object oggetto
object (to) obiettare
obnoxious odioso, disgustoso
obtain (to) ottenere
obvious ovvio
occasion occasione
occasionally occasionalmente
occupied occupato
occupy (to) occupare
ocean oceano
October ottobre
octopus polipo, piovra
oculist oculista
odd dispari; strano
of di
of course certamente
off spento, da lontano, via, remoto
offence offesa
offend (to) offendere, offendersi
offer offerta

offer (to) offrire
office ufficio
often spesso
oil olio, greggio
ointment unguento
old vecchio
olive oliva
omelet frittata
on su; acceso
once una volta, un tempo
one uno
oneself se stesso
onion cipolla
only solo
open aperto
open (to) aprire
operation operazione
operator operatore
opinion opinione
opportunity opportunità
opposite opposto; di fronte (a)
oral orale
orange arancia
order ordine
order (to) ordinare
ordinary ordinario
organization organizzazione
organize (to) organizzare
originate (to) originare, generare
orphan orfano
other altro
otherwise altrimenti
our nostro
out esterno, fuori
outside fuori, all'aperto
oval ovale
oven forno
over oltre, finito, su
owe (to) dovere (a qualcuno), essere in debito

owl gufo
owner proprietario
ownership proprietà
oxygen ossigeno
oyster ostrica

P

pace passo
Pacific Pacifico
pack (to) fare i bagagli, impacchettare
package imballaggio, pacco
page pagina
pain dolore, pena
painkiller antidolorifico
paint (to) dipingere
paintbrush pennello
painter pittore
painting quadro, pittura
pair paio
pajamas pigiama
palace palazzo
pale pallido
palm palmo, palma
palpitation palpitazione
panic panico
panic (to) farsi prendere dal panico
panties *(pl.)* mutandine
pantry dispensa
paper carta
paperback libro in brossura
paprika paprica
paradise paradiso
paralyze (to) paralizzare
paralysis paralisi
parcel pacco
parents *(pl.)* genitori
parish parrocchia

park parco
parking posteggio auto
parliament parlamento
parsley prezzemolo
part *n.* parte
participate (to) partecipare
participation partecipazione
partner partner, compagno, socio
party festa
pass (to) passare
passage passaggio
passenger passeggero
passion passione
passport passaporto
past passato
pastry pasticceria, paste *pl.*
path sentiero, pista
patience pazienza
patient paziente
patrol pattuglia
pay (to) pagare
payment pagamento
pea pisello
peace pace
peaceful pacifico
peach pesca
peak picco, altura
peanut arachide
pear pera
pearl perla
peasant contadino
pedal pedale
pen penna
penalty penalità, multa
pencil matita
penguin pinguino
penis pene
pension pensione
people *(pl.)* gente *s.*

pepper pepe
percentage percentuale
perfect perfetto
perform (to) eseguire, esibirsi
performance esibizione
perfume profumo
perhaps forse
period periodo
perish (to) perire
permanent permanente
permission permesso
permit permesso
permit (to) permettere
persist (to) persistere
persistence persistenza
persistent persistente
personal personale
perspiration sudorazione, traspirazione
petroleum petrolio
pharmacy farmacia
philosophy filosofia
phone telefono
phone booth cabina telefonica
photocopy fotocopia
photograph fotografia
phrase frase
physics fisica
piano pianoforte
pick (to) raccogliere
picture fotografia; immagine
piece pezzo, parte
pig maiale
pigeon piccione
pill pillola
pillow cuscino
pillowcase federa
pilot pilota
pin spillo
pine (tree) pino

pineapple ananas
pink rosa
pipe tubo
pity pietà, pena
place posto, luogo
place (to) mettere, piazzare
plain piano, chiaro, evidente
plan piano
plan (to) pianificare
plane aereo
plant pianta
plant (to) piantare
plastic plastica
plate piatto
play gioco; pièce teatrale
play (to) suonare; recitare; giocare
player attore, suonatore, musicista
please per favore
please (to) far piacere, compiacere
pleasure piacere
plentiful abbondante
plenty pieno, in abbondanza
plug tappo, spina
plug (to) inserire la spina
plum prugna, susina
pneumonia polmonite
pocket tasca
poem poesia
poison veleno
poisoning avvelenamento
poisonous velenoso
Poland Polonia
police polizia
policeman poliziotto
Polish polacco
polite educato
polluted inquinato
poor povero
populace popolo, popolazione

popular popolare
porcelain porcellana
porch portico
pork porco
porter portiere
portion porzione
possession possesso
possibility possibilità
possible possibile
postcard cartolina
post office ufficio postale
potato patata
pottery terraglie
poultry pollame
pound libbra, sterlina
pour (to) versare
poverty povertà
power potere
praise (to) elogiare, lodare
pray (to) pregare
precaution precauzione
precise preciso
pregnant gravida, incinta
prehistoric preistorico
prepare (to) preparare
prescribe (to) prescrivere
prescription ricetta
present regalo
present (to) presentare
pressure pressione
pretend (to) fingere
pretty grazioso
price prezzo
pride orgoglio
priest prete, sacerdote
prince principe
princess principessa
prison prigione
private privato

probably probabilmente
problem problema
process processo
produce (to) produrre
production produzione
profession professione
professor professore
profit profitto
profitable redditizio
program programma
prohibit (to) proibire
promise promessa
pronunciation pronuncia
proof prova
proper appropriato, a modo
proposal proposta
protect (to) proteggere
protection protezione
protestant protestante
proud orgoglioso
prove (to) provare, dare prova
proverb proverbio
public pubblico
pull (to) tirare
pullover pullover, maglione
pulse polso, pulsazione
pump pompa
pumpkin zucca
punishment punizione
pupil scolaro
purchase acquisto
purple purpureo, paonazzo
purse borsetta
push (to) spingere

Q

qualification qualifica, qualificazione
qualified qualificato

qualify (to) qualificare
quality qualità
quantity quantità
quarrel (to) discutere, litigare
quarter quarto, quartiere
queen regina
question domanda, questione
queue fila
queue (to) fare la fila, stare in fila
quick svelto, lesto, rapido
quickly velocemente
quiet quieto, tranquillo, zitto
quintet quintetto
quit (to) lasciare, abbandonare
quite interamente, piuttosto
quotation citazione
quote (to) citare

R

rabbi rabbino
rabbit coniglio
race (human) razza
racket missile
radiator radiatore
radio radio
radish ravanello
rag straccio
railroad ferrovia
rain pioggia
rain (to) piovere
rainbow arcobaleno
raincoat impermeabile
raise (to) alzare, alzarsi, crescere
raisin uva passa
rare raro
raspberry lampone
rat ratto

rate tasso, quota, tariffa
rather piuttosto
raw crudo, grezzo
razor rasoio
read (to) leggere
ready pronto
really realmente, veramente
rear posteriore, retro
reason ragione; raziocinio
recall (to) ricordare, rievocare
receipt ricevuta
receive (to) ricevere
receiver ricevitore
reception ricezione, ricevimento
recipe ricetta
recognize (to) riconoscere
recollection ricordo
recommend (to) raccomandare
recommendation raccomandazione
recover (to) guarire, recuperare
recovery guarigione, ripresa
red rosso
reduction riduzione
reflect (to) riflettere
reflection riflessione
refresh (to) rinfrescare, rinfrescarsi
refreshment rinfresco, ristoro
refugee rifugiato
refund (to) rimborsare
refusal rifiuto
refuse (to) rifiutare
regard (to) riguardare, concernere
regarding riguardo a
regards (my) *(pl.)* i miei riguardi
region regione
register (to) registrare, iscrivere, iscriversi
registration iscrizione
regular *adj.* regolare
regularly regolarmente

rejoice (to) esultare, rallegrarsi
relationship relazione
relative *n.* parente; *adj.* relativo
relax (to) rilassarsi
relief sollievo, aiuto
religion religione
religious religioso
reluctant riluttante
remain (to) rimanere
remember (to) ricordare
rent affitto
rent (to) affittare
repair (to) riparare
repeat (to) ripetere
report rapporto, resoconto
representative rappresentativo
repugnant ripugnante
request richiesta
request (to) richiedere
rescue (to) salvare, soccorrere
research ricerca
research (to) ricercare
resemblance rassomiglianza
reservation prenotazione
reserve (to) prenotare
reside (to) risiedere
residence residenza
respect rispetto
respect (to) rispettare
respectable rispettabile
responsibility responsabilità
responsible responsabile
rest resto, riposo
rest (to) riposare
restaurant ristorante
restructure (to) ristrutturare
return ritorno
return (to) ritornare
return ticket (biglietto) andata e ritorno

reveal (to) rivelare
revenge vendetta
rheumatism reumatismi *pl.*
rib costola
ribbon fiocco
rice riso
rich ricco
ride (to) percorrere con un mezzo, guidare
ridiculous ridicolo
right destra, giusto
ring anello
ring (to) suonare
rival rivale
river fiume
road strada
road sign segnale stradale
robber ladro
robbery furto
robe veste
rock pietra
roof tetto
room stanza
rosary rosario
rose rosa
rotten marcio
round giro; rotondo
route percorso, strada
row fila
rubber mastice
rug tappetino, coperta
ruin rovina
ruin (to) rovinare
ruined rovinato
run corsa; gita
run (to) correre
Russia Russia
Russian russo
rust ruggine
rye segale

S

sad triste
sadly tristemente
safe sicuro, salvo
safety sicurezza
saffron zafferano
sage salvia (*bot.*); saggio, dotto
sail (to) navigare
saint santo
salad insalata
salary salario
salmon salmone
salt sale
same stesso, medesimo
sand sabbia
sandal sandalo
sandwich panino
sanitary napkin assorbente femminile
sardine sardina
satisfied soddisfatto
satisfy (to) soddisfare
saturate (to) saturare
Saturday sabato
sauce sugo
saucepan casseruola
sausage salsiccia
save (to) salvare
say (to) dire
scale bilancia
scallop conchiglia
scarf sciarpa
schedule catalogo, inventario
scholarship dottrina; borsa di studio
school scuola
science scienza
scientist scienziato
scissors *(pl.)* forbici

Scotland Scozia
Scottish scozzese
scream (to) urlare, gridare
sculptor scultore
sculpture scultura
sea mare
seafood frutti di mare
search (to) ricercare
season stagione
seat belt cintura di sicurezza
second secondo
secondhand di seconda mano, usato
secret segreto
secretly segretamente
see (to) vedere
seem (to) sembrare
seldom raramente
self sé, l'io
self-esteem auto-stima
sell (to) vendere
send (to) spedire, inviare
sense senso, significato
sensitive sensibile, suscettibile
sentence frase
separate (to) separare
separation separazione
September settembre
serious serio
serve (to) servire
service servizio
session sessione
seven sette
seventeen diciassette
seventy settanta
several diversi, numerosi
sew (to) cucire
sex sesso
shadow ombra
shake (to) scuotere, agitare

shallow basso, superficiale
shame vergogna
share (to) dividere, condividere
shark squalo
sharp affilato, appuntito
sharpen (to) affilare, aguzzare
shave (to) sbarbare, radere
she ella
sheep pecora, ovino
sheet foglio; lenzuolo
shelf scaffale
shell conchiglia, guscio
shine (to) brillare, splendere
shirt camicia
shoe scarpa
shoot (to) sparare
shop negozio
shop (to) fare compere
shore costa, spiaggia
short corto, breve
shortage carenza, penuria
shorten (to) accorciare
shoulder spalla
shout (to) gridare, urlare
show spettacolo
show (to) mostrare
shower doccia
shrimp gamberetto
shy timido, riservato
sick malato
sickness malattia
side lato, fianco, parte
sidewalk marciapiede
sigh sospiro
sigh (to) sospirare
sight vista
sightseeing visita guidata, giro turistico
sign segno, segnale
signature firma

silence silenzio
silk seta
silver argento
similar simile, analogo
simple semplice
simply semplicemente
sin peccato
sin (to) peccare
since da quando, da allora in poi
sincerity sincerità
sing (to) cantare
singer cantante
sink lavandino
sister sorella
sister-in-law cognata
sit (to) sedere
situation situazione
six sei
size misura, grandezza
skate (to) pattinare
skis *(pl.)* sci
ski (to) sciare
skill attitudine, abilità
skin pelle
skirt gonna
sky cielo
sleep (to) dormire
sleepless insonne
sleeve manica
slide (to) scivolare
slim magro, sottile
small piccolo
smart intelligente, acuto
smell olfatto, odore
smell (to) odorare
smile sorriso
smile (to) sorridere
smoke fumo
smoke (to) fumare

smoker fumatore
smooth liscio, levigato
snake serpente
sneeze (to) starnutire
snore (to) russare
snow neve
snow (to) nevicare
so così
soap sapone
sober sobrio, composto
society società
socks *(pl.)* pedalini, calzettoni
soft morbido
solitude solitudine
some alcuni, qualche
somehow in qualche modo
someone qualcuno
something qualcosa
sometime(s) qualche volta, a volte
somewhere in qualche luogo, da qualche parte
son figlio
song canzone
son-in-law genero
soon presto
sorrow dolore, dispiacere
sorry! Mi spiace! Scusi!
soul anima
soup zuppa, minestra
sour acido, acerbo, aspro
South Sud
Southern meridionale
souvenir souvenir, ricordo
Spain Spagna
Spanish spagnolo
spark scintilla, favilla
sparrow passero
speak (to) parlare
special speciale
speech discorso

speed velocità
spell (to) sillabare
spend (to) spendere, passare (il tempo)
spice spezia, aroma
spinach spinaci *pl.*
spirit spirito
spiritual spirituale
splendor splendore
spoil (to) viziare
spoiled viziato
spoon cucchiaio
spot macchia; località
spring primavera
spy spia
square piazza
stab (to) accoltellare, pugnalare
stained macchiato, sporco
stair scalino, gradino
staircase scala
stamp francobollo
stand (to) stare in piedi, trovarsi
star stella
starch amido
start (to) iniziare, cominciare, avviare
startle (to) trasalire
state stato
station stazione
statue statua
stay permanenza
stay (to) rimanere, restare
steak bistecca
steal (to) rubare
steam vapore
steel acciaio
step passo
stew stufato, umido
still fermo, immobile, morto
sting pungiglione, aculeo
stink (to) puzzare

stir (to) rimescolare
stock provvista; azione in borsa
stocking calza
stomach stomaco
stone pietra
stop (to) fermare, fermarsi
store negozio
stork cicogna
storm temporale, tempesta
story storia
stove macchina del gas, stufa
straight dritto
strange strano
stranger straniero
straw paglia
strawberry fragola
stream corso, flusso, ruscello
street strada
strengthen (to) rinforzare
stress (to) sottolineare
strict stretto, ligio, esatto
strike sciopero
strong forte
student studente
study (to) studiare
stuffing imbottitura, ripieno
stupid stupido
subject soggetto
suburb sobborgo
succeed (to) avere successo, riuscire
success successo, riuscita
sudden improvviso
suffer (to) soffrire
sugar zucchero
suicide suicidio
suitable adatto
suitcase valigia
summer estate
sun sole

sunbathe (to) prendere il sole
Sunday domenica
sunglasses *(pl.)* occhiali da sole
sunny assolato
supper cena
support sostegno
support (to) sostenere
suppose (to) supporre
sure sicuro, certo
surely sicuramente
surface superficie
surgeon chirurgo
surgery chirurgia
surname cognome
surprise sorpresa
surprise (to) sorprendere
suspicious sospettoso
swallow (to) ingoiare
swear (to) giurare
sweat sudore
sweat (to) sudare
sweater maglione
sweet dolce
sweets *(pl.)* dolci
swim (to) nuotare
swimmer nuotatore
swimming pool piscina
swimsuit costume da bagno
Swiss svizzero
switch (to) accendere, scambiare
Switzerland Svizzera
symphony sinfonia
synthetic sintetico
system sistema

T

table tavolino, tavola
tablet pastiglia, compressa

tailor sarto
take (to) prendere
tale favola, storia
talent talento
talk conversazione
talk (to) parlare, conversare
tampon tampone
tan *n.* abbronzatura
tangerine mandarino
tape nastro
taste sapore
taste (to) assaporare, assaggiare
tasty saporito
tax tassa
tea tè
teach (to) insegnare
teacher insegnante
tear (drop) lacrima
teaspoon cucchiaino
tedious tedioso
telegram telegramma
telephone telefono
telephone call telefonata
television televisione
tell (to) dire, raccontare
temperature temperatura, febbre
temporary temporaneo
ten dieci
tenderness tenerezza
tent tenda
tenth decimo
terrace terrazza
terrible terribile
territory territorio
terror terrore
testify (to) testimoniare
tetanus tetano
than che, di quello che
thank (to) ringraziare

Thank you! Grazie!

that quello, quel, quella, che

theater teatro

theft ladro

then allora, poi

there là, lì, ci, vi

therefore perciò, dunque, pertanto

thermometer termometro

thick spesso, erto

thigh coscia

thin magro

thing cosa

think (to) pensare

third terzo

thirst sete

thirsty assetato

thirty trenta

thousand mille

thread filo

threat minaccia

threaten (to) minacciare

three tre

throat gola

through attraverso, per

throw (to) gettare

thunder tuono

Thursday giovedì

thyme timo

ticket biglietto

tide marea

tie legame, laccio, cravatta

tie (to) legare, allacciare

tight stretto

time tempo, ora

timely opportuno

tip mancia; cima

tip (to) dare la mancia, battere

tissue tessuto

tobacconist tabaccaio

today oggi
toe dito del piede
together insieme
tolerant tollerante
tomato pomodoro
tomb tomba
tomorrow domani
tongue lingua
tonight stanotte, stasera
tonsil tonsilla
too anche, troppo
tooth dente
toothache mal di denti
toothbrush spazzolino da denti
toothpaste dentifricio
toothpick stuzzicadenti
torture tortura
torture (to) torturare
touch tocco
touch (to) toccare
tough duro, robusto, inflessibile
tourist turista
toward(s) verso
towel asciugamano
tower torre
town città
toy giocattolo
track traccia, sentiero, binario
tradition tradizione
traditional tradizionale
traffic traffico
traffic light semaforo
train treno
trait tratto, caratteristica
traitor traditore
tranquilizer calmante, tranquillante
transfer (to) trasferire
translate (to) tradurre
translation traduzione

translator traduttore
transport (to) trasportare
transportation trasporto
travel viaggio
travel (to) viaggiare
traveler viaggiatore
treat (to) trattare
tree albero
tremendous tremendo
trip viaggio, escursione
trolley filobus, tram
trousers *(pl.)* pantaloni
trout trota
true vero
truly francamente, veramente
trumpet tromba
truth verità
try (to) provare
Tuesday martedì
tumor tumore
tuna tonno
turkey tacchino
Turkish turco
turn (to) girare, svoltare
turquoise turchese
twice due volte
twin gemello
twins *(pl.)* gemelli
type tipo
typewriter macchina da scrivere

U

ugly brutto
ulcer ulcera
umbrella ombrello
unbelievable incredibile
uncertain incerto

uncle zio
uncomfortable scomodo
unconscious incosciente
unconsciousness incoscienza
under sotto
understand (to) capire
understanding comprensione
undertaking impresa
underwear intimo, biancheria intima
undress (to) spogliarsi
unemployed disoccupato
unfit inadatto, inabile
unfold (to) schiudere, svelare, svelarsi
unfortunately sfortunatamente
unhappiness infelicità
unhappy infelice
unhealthy non salubre, malsano
uninterested disinteressato
unite (to) unirsi
United States *(pl.)* Stati Uniti
universe universo
university università
unjust ingiusto
unkind scortese
unknown sconosciuto
unlawful illegale
unnecessary gratuito, non richiesto
unofficial ufficioso
unpack (to) disfare i bagagli
unpleasant spiacevole, sgradevole
unpopular impopolare
unqualified non qualificato
unreal irreale
unreasonable irragionevole
unreliable inaffidabile
unrest inquietudine
unstable instabile
until fino (a)
untrue falso, infedele

unusual inusuale, insolito
up su, in su, in alto
upbringing educazione, crescita
upper superiore
upset rovesciato, sconvolto
upset (to) sconvolgere, rovesciare
upstairs al piano di sopra
up-to-date aggiornato
urban urbano
urgent urgente
urgently urgentemente
urinate (to) urinare
urine urina
use uso
use (to) usare
useful utile
useless inutile
usher usciere, valletto
usual usuale, solito
utensil utensile
uterus utero
utmost maggiore, massimo
U-turn inversione a U

V

vacancy disponibilità
vacant libero, vuoto
vacation vacanza
vaccinate (to) vaccinare
vacuum cleaner aspirapolvere
vaginal vaginale
vague vago
vain vano
valid valido
valley valle
value valore
vandal vandalo

vandalism vandalismo
variety varietà
various alcuni, molti
vase vaso
Vatican Vaticano
veal vitello
vegetable verdura
vehicle veicolo
veil velo
vein vena
verb verbo
verse verso, strofa
version versione
very molto
veterinary veterinario
victim vittima
victory vittoria
view vista
vile vile
village villaggio
vinegar aceto
vineyard vigneto, vigna
violence violenza
violent violento
violin violino
virtue virtù
visa visto
visible visibile
vision visione
visit visita
visit (to) visitare
vitamin vitamina
vocabulary vocabolario
voice voce
voltage voltaggio
volunteer volontario
vomit (to) vomitare, rimettere
vote voto
vote (to) votare

voucher documento, attestato
vowel vocale
voyage viaggio
vulgar volgare

W

wages *(pl.)* salario *s.*
wagon vagone
wait (to) aspettare, attendere
waiter cameriere
waitress cameriera
wake veglia
wake up (to) svegliarsi
walk passeggiata, cammino
walk (to) camminare, passeggiare
wall parete, muro
wallet portafoglio
walnut noce
wander (to) vagabondare
want (to) volere
war guerra
wardrobe guardaroba
warm caldo
warmth calore
wash (to) lavare
waste spreco
waste (to) sprecare
watch orologio
watch (to) guardare
watchmaker orologiaio
water acqua
waterfall cascata
wave onda
way via, direzione
we noi
weak debole
weakness debolezza

weapon arma
weather tempo atmosferico
wedding matrimonio
Wednesday mercoledì
week settimana
weekend fine settimana
weigh (to) pesare
weight peso
Welcome! Benvenuto!
well *adj.* bene; *n.* pozzo
West Ovest, occidente
Western occidentale
wet bagnato
whale balena
what che cosa
wheel ruota
when quando
whenever quandunque
where dove
whether se
which il quale
whisper sussurro
whisper (to) sussurrare
whistle (to) fischiare
white bianco
who chi
whole intero, tutto
whose di chi, del quale
why perché
wide ampio, largo, spalancato
widow vedova
widower vedovo
width larghezza
wife moglie
wild *n., adj.* selvaggio, *adj.* selvatico
will volontà; testamento
will (to) volere
win (to) vincere
wind vento

window finestra
wine vino
wing ala
winter inverno
wise saggio
wish desiderio, augurio
wish (to) augurare
with con
withdraw (to) ritirare
without senza
witness testimone
wolf lupo
woman donna
wonder meraviglia
wonderful meraviglioso
wood legno
wool lana
word parola
work lavoro
work (to) lavorare
worker lavoratore, operaio
world mondo
worry preoccupazione
worry (to) preoccuparsi
worsen (to) peggiorare
write (to) scrivere
writer scrittore
wrong sbagliato, erroneo
wrong (to be) aver torto

X

xenophobia xenofobia
x-rays *(pl.)* raggi x

Y

yacht yacht, panfilo
yard iarda, cortile
yawn (to) sbadigliare
year anno
yearly annualmente
yearn (to) languire, bramare
yeast lievito, fermento
yell (to) urlare, strillare
yellow giallo
yes si
yesterday ieri
yet ancora, già, tuttavia
yogurt yogurt
yolk tuorlo
you tu
young giovane
yourself te stesso
youth gioventù

Z

zeal zelo
zebra zebra
zero zero
zest aroma, gusto
zinc zinco
zipper cerniera lampo
Zionist sionista
zone zona
zoo zoo
zoological zoologico
zoology zoologia

ITALIAN PHRASEBOOK

1. GREETINGS & POLITENESS

Good morning! **Buon giorno!**
Good evening! **Buona sera!**
Good night! **Buona notte!**
Hi! **Salve!**
Hello! **Ciao!**
Bye-bye! **Ciao!**
So long! **Arrivederci!**
See you soon/later! **A presto!**
Good-bye! **Addio!**

How are you? **Come sta?** (formal)
                    Come stai? (informal)
                    Come va? (informal)

Fine, thank you. **Bene, grazie.**
Very well, and you? **Molto bene, e Lei?**

I feel great, thanks, and you? **Sto benissimo, grazie, e tu?**
Not so bad, thanks. **Non c'è male, grazie.**
So-so. **Così così.**

Nice to meet you. **Piacere di conoscerLa./Piacere.**

2. GETTING ALONG

Do you speak English? **Parla inglese?**

I don't speak Italian. **Io non parlo italiano.**

I can also speak French, and you? **Io parlo anche francese, e Lei?**

Please, speak slowly; my Italian isn't good. **Per favore, può parlare più lentamente? Il mio italiano non è buono.**

Do you understand my English? **Mi capisce se parlo inglese?**

Can you write down for me how to say that in Italian? **Può scrivermi come si dice in Italiano?**

Can you write it down on a piece of paper, please? **Può scrivermelo su un pezzo di carta?**

Does anyone speak English here? **C'è nessuno che parli inglese qui?**

Is there an interpreter? **C'è un interprete?**

I have to look it up in my dictionary. **Devo cercare nel dizionario.**

How do you say in Italian…? **Come si dice in Italiano …?**

3. ASKING FOR DIRECTIONS

Can you tell me the way to...? **Può dirmi qual'è la strada per...?**

How do I get to…? **Come si va a...?**

Are we on the right road for…? **Siamo sulla strada giusta per ...?**

How far is the next village? **Quanto dista il prossimo villaggio?**

How far is ...... from here? **Quanto dista...da qui?**

Is there an expressway? **C'è un'autostrada?**

How long does it take by car? **Quanto tempo ci vuole in macchina?**

Can I drive through the town center? **Si può andare in macchina nel centro-città?**

The town center is closed to cars. **Il centro è zona pedonale.**

Can you tell me where …is? **Può dirmi dove si trova ...?**

How can I find this address? **Dove posso trovare questo indirizzo?**

Could you show me on the map where I am? **Può indicarmi sulla carta dove mi trovo?**

Turn left. **Giri a sinistra.**

Turn right. **Giri a destra.**

Go straight ahead. **Vada dritto.**

After the bridge, turn… **Dopo il ponte, giri a...**

At the first traffic light. **Al primo semaforo.**

The second on your right. **La seconda a destra.**

The third on your left. **La terza a sinistra.**

Go straight, at the second traffic light turn… **Vada dritto, al secondo semaforo giri a…**

Make a U-turn. **Faccia un'inversione a U.**

Go to the first intersection. **Vada fino al primo incrocio.**

Turn left/right at the next corner. **Giri a sinistra/destra al prossimo angolo.**

ASKING FOR DIRECTIONS

Follow the sign for "Rome". **Segua le indicazioni per Roma.**

You have to go back! **Deve tornare indietro!**

You are going the wrong way! **Lei è sulla strada sbagliata.**

I am sorry, I am a stranger myself. **Mi dispiace, non sono pratico della zona.**

It's not far. **Non è lontano.**

It's close from here. **È vicino.**

It's down there... **È laggiù...**

It's a five minute walk. **È a cinque minuti a piedi.**

on the left **a sinistra**

on the right **a destra**

opposite **di fronte**

behind **dietro**

next to **accanto a**

after **dopo**

north of **a nord di**

south **a sud**

eastward **verso est**

westward **verso ovest**

on foot **a piedi**

by car **in macchina**

4. TRAVEL & TRANSPORTATION

Driving in Italy - In machina

On the Italian **autostrada** (expressway) you have to pay a **pedaggio** (tolls) at the **caselli** (toll booths).

Gas station - Benzinaio

Where is the nearest gas station, please? **Dov'è il benzinaio più vicino, per favore?**
Full tank, please. **Mi faccia il pieno, per favore.**
Give me five liters of petrol. **Mi dia cinque litri di benzina.**
Ten liters of gas/petrol, please. **Mi mette dieci litri di benzina, per favore?**

half tank **mezzo serbatoio**
super, premium **super**
regular, standard **normale**
unleaded **senza piombo**
diesel **gasolio/diesel**

Repairs - Autoriparazioni

Please, check the... **Per favore, controlli …**
Would you check the tire pressure? **Può controllare la pressione delle gomme?**
Please, check the spare tire, too. **Per favore, controlli anche la ruota di scorta.**

garage **autorimessa**
mechanic **meccanico**
body work and electrical repairs **carrozzeria/elettrauto**
battery **la batteria**
brake fluid **l'olio dei freni**
oil/water **l'olio/l'acqua**

Car parts - Pezzi/parti della macchina

indicators **frecce (o lampeggiatori)**
brakes **freni**
wipers **i tergicristalli**
gear box **il cambio**
fan belt **la cinghia del ventilatore**
clutch **la frizione**
tire **la gomma**
bulb **la lampadina**
spark plugs **le candele**
steering **lo sterzo**
lights **le luci**
engine **il motore**
fuel pump **pompa della benzina**
radiator **il radiatore**
heater **sistema di riscaldamento**
exhaust pipe **tubo di scappamento**

Parking - Parcheggio

Where can I park? **Dove posso parcheggiare?**
Is there a car park nearby? **C'è un parcheggio qui vicino?**
May I park here? **Posso parcheggiare qui?**
How long can I park here? **Quanto tempo posso restare qui?**
What's the rate per hour? **Quanto si paga l'ora?**
Is this a free parking lot? **È un parcheggio libero?**

Road signs - Segnali stradali

Accendere i fari in galleria Switch on the headlights before entering tunnel
Accostare a destra/sinistra Keep right/left
Alt Stop

Area di servizio Service area
Caduta massi Falling rocks
Carabinieri Police
Circonvallazione Belt highway
Corsia d'emergenza Emergency parking zone
Curve per 5 km Bends for 5 Km
Deviazione Diversion/detour
Divieto Di Sorpasso No Overtaking Passing
Divieto Di Sosta No Parking
Lavori in corso Road works ahead
Passaggio a livello Level railroad crossing
Pericolo Danger
Polizia stradale Highway police
Rallentare Reduce speed
Senso Unico One Way
Soccorso A.C.I. Emergency road service
Strada dissestata Poor road surface
Strada senza uscita Dead end road
Vietato l'Accesso No Entry
Vigili urbani City police
Zona pedonale Pedestrian zone

On the bus - Sull'autobus

Which bus takes me to the Colosseum? **Che auto devo prendere per il Colosseo?**
Where is the bus stop? **Dov'è la fermata dell'auto?**
Excuse me, is this the right bus to Saint Peter? **Mi scusi, è questo l'auto per San Pietro?**
Where do I get the bus to...? **Dove prendo l'auto per…?**
One (bus) ticket, please. **Vorrei un biglietto dell'auto.**
I have to get off at... **Devo scendere a…**
Can you tell me where to get off? **Sa dirmi dove devo scendere?**

At the train station - Alla stazione

When is the next train to...? **Quand'è il prossimo treno per...?**

I'd like to buy a return ticket. **Vorrei un biglietto di andata e ritorno.**

A one-way ticket, please. **Un biglietto di sola andata.**

Do you have special student fares? **Ci sono sconti per gli studenti?**

First class, please. **Un biglietto di prima classe, grazie.**

At what time does the train arrive in...? **A che ora arriva il treno a…?**

Is it a local? **È un diretto?**

Is it an express? **È un espresso?**

May I have a timetable, please? **Posso avere un orario dei treni?**

From which platform does it leave? **Da quale binario parte il treno?**

Is there a dining car? **C'è un vagone ristorante?**

May I reserve a sleeping cabin? **Posso prenotare una cuccetta?**

The train for Rome leaves at... **Il treno per Roma parte alle...**

The train arrives in Florence at... **Il treno arriva a Firenze alle...**

You need a reservation for this train. **È un treno con prenotazione obbligatoria.**

You must pay a supplement. **Deve pagare un supplemento.**

All sleeping cabins are non-smoking. **Tutte le cuccette sono non-fumatori.**

The train leaves from platform... **Il treno parte dal binario...**

When you get to... ask the conductor. **Quando arriva a... chieda al conducente.**

The port - Al porto

Among the many attractions of Italy, its marvelous islands play a central role: Sicily, Sardinia, Capri, just to mention a few, are considered an earthly paradise by tourists from all over the world and Italians alike. To reach these places you will have to take a ferry. Here is a list of useful words for sea travel.

ferry **traghetto**
ship **nave**
boat **battello**
passage **traversata**
cruise **crociera**
seaport **porto**
pier, dock **molo**
quay **banchina**
car passage (the ticket to board the car on the ship)
      passaggio auto
passenger **passeggero**
life-boat **scialuppa di salvataggio**
captain, master, skipper **capitano**
mariner, seaman **marinaio**
harbor master's office **capitaneria di porto**
passenger's cabin **cabina**
deckhouse **cabina di coperta**
deck **ponte**
docking **attracco**
to weigh anchor **salpare (l'ancora)**
to leave the port **lasciare il porto**
home port **porto d'armamento**
to enter port **entrare in porto**
port of call **porto di scalo**
to call at a port **fare scalo ad un porto**
(pilot) bridge **plancia**
stern **poppa**
afterdeck **ponte di poppa**
gangplank **passerella**
mainmast **albero maestro**
seasickness **mal di mare**

5. ACCOMMODATION

Good morning, are there still vacancies in your hotel?
Buon giorno, avete camere disponibili nel vostro albergo?

I'd like to book a room for two for just one night.
Vorrei prenotare una stanza per due persone, per una notte.

I'd like a double room with bathroom. **Vorrei una doppia con bagno.**

We would like a room with a double bed and a shower.
Vorremmo una matrimoniale con doccia.

I need a single room for two nights. **Vorrei una singola per due notti.**

We don't know yet how long we are going to stay. **Non sappiamo ancora quanto rimarremo.**

We are on our honeymoon. Is it possible to have a room with a view? **Siamo in viaggio di nozze. È possibile avere una camera con vista?**

Is breakfast included? **La colazione è inclusa?**

Has the room got air-conditioning/tv/telephone/bath?
La stanza è con aria condizionata/televisione/telefono/bagno?

Have you got discounts for students/senior citizens?
Fate sconti per gli studenti/anziani?

How much is a double without bath? **Quanto costa una doppia senza bagno?**

Can we see the room? **Possiamo vedere la stanza?**

Does the hotel organize sightseeing tours of the city?
Il vostro hotel organizza tours della città?

Is there a shuttle bus from the hotel to the airport? **C'è un autobus che parte dall'hotel per l'aeroporto?**

At what time and how often does it leave? **A che ora parte e con quale frequenza?**

At what time does the hotel restaurant close/open? **A che ora chiude/apre il ristorante dell'hotel?**

Is it possible to have kosher food at the hotel restaurant?
È possibile avere un menu kosher nel ristorante dell'albergo?

Are there any messages for me? **Ci sono telefonate/messaggi per me?**

We still have many vacancies. **Abbiamo ancora molte stanze disponibili.**

I am sorry, we haven't got any room left. **Mi dispiace non abbiamo più stanze disponibili.**

When would you need the room? **Per quando vi serve la stanza?**

For how many nights? **Per quante notti?**

We have two rooms available, a double with bath and a single room without bath. **Abbiamo disponibili due stanze, una doppia con bagno e una singola senza bagno.**

All rooms are non-smoking. **Non è permesso fumare in nessuna delle nostre camere.**

Breakfast is/isn't included. **La colazione è/non è inclusa nel prezzo.**

Here is your key. **Ecco le chiavi della stanza.**

You can take it with you when you leave the hotel. **Potete portarle con voi.**

You must leave the keys at the reception when you go out of the hotel. **Dovete lasciare le chiavi alla consiergerie quando uscite dall'albergo.**

The hotel restaurant opens at 7 in the morning and closes at 9 in the evening. **Il ristorante dell'albergo apre la mattina alle 7 e chiude la sera alle 9.**

We accept only cash or credit card payments. **Qui si accettano solo contante o carta di credito.**

A shuttle bus to the airport leaves the hotel every hour daily. **Ogni giorno un autobus parte dall'hotel ogni ora e va all'aeroporto.**

It's a free service. **È un servizio gratuito.**

Sir/Madam, someone called today and left this message for you. **Signore/Signora, qualcuno ha chiamato per Lei oggi ed ha lasciato questo messaggio.**

6. FOOD & DRINK

At the café - Al bar

What can we have at the café? **Cosa prendiamo al bar?**

To drink - Da bere

coffee **un caffé**
cappuccino **un cappuccino**
coffee with milk **un caffellatte**
iced cappuccino **un cappuccino freddo**
less strong coffee **un caffé lungo**
double espresso **un caffé doppio**
coffee with a drop of milk **un caffé macchiato**
very strong coffee **un caffé ristretto**
coffee with a drop of liqueur **un caffé corretto**
decaffeinated coffee **un caffé decaffeinato**
tea **un té**
iced tea **un té freddo**
decaffeinated tea **un té deteinato**
hot milk **un latte caldo**
fruit juice **un succo di frutta**
lemon juice, lemonade **una limonata**
a glass of water **un bicchiere d'acqua semplice**
mineral water **un bicchiere d'acqua minerale**
natural (non-sparkling) water **aqua naturale**
tap water **acqua semplice di rubinetto**

To eat - Da mangiare

croissant **un cornetto**
croissant with whipped cream **un cornetto con la panna**
Sicilian crescent **un cannolo (siciliano)**
doughnut **una ciambella**
cream doughnut **una bomba (alla crema)**
(ham, cheese) sandwich **un tramezzino (al prosciutto, al formaggio)**

What would you like, Madam? **Cosa desidera, Signora?**
What will you have, Sir? **Cosa prende, Signore?**
For you, Madam? **Per Lei, Signora?**

I'd like a coffee, please. **Vorrei un caffé, per piacere.**
Tea for me, please. **Per me un té, per favore.**
I'll have a cappuccino, please. **Prendo un cappuccino,**
    grazie.

How much is it? **Quant'è?**
How much does it cost? **Quanto costa?**

At the restaurant - Al ristorante/in trattoria

Menu - Menu

appetizers **antipasti**
main dish **primi piatti**
second course **secondi piatti**
side dish **contorno**
dessert **dolce**
fruits **frutta**
beverages **bevande**

dish of the day **piatto del giorno**
the chef recommends **lo chef consiglia**
specialties of the house **specialità della casa**

Pizze - Pizza

Margherita tomato, mozzarella
Capricciosa tomato, mozzarella, capers, mushrooms
Napoletana tomato, mozzarella, anchovies
Quattro stagioni tomato, mozzarella, mushrooms,
    ham, olives
Siciliana tomato, black olives, capers and cheese
Quattro formaggi four cheeses, no tomato

Fiori di zucca no tomato, mozzarella, zucchini flowers
Funghi tomato, mozzarella, mushrooms
Con la rughetta basic pizza with arugula salad on top
Al gorgonzola pizza with blue cheese
Prosciutto ham pizza
Crostino round-cut French bread with mozzarella on
    top (from the brick oven)
Crostino alle alici round-cut French bread topped with
    mozzarella and anchovies
Crostino al prosciutto round-cut French bread topped
    with mozzarella and ham
Calzone cheese, ham or sausage calzone
Supplí fried rice ball filled with mozzarella

Minestre - Soups

Minestra del giorno soup of the day
Minestrone Italian all-vegetables-soup
Pasta e fagioli short-pasta-and-beans soup
Minestra in brodo soup-bouillon with noodles or rice
Zuppa alla marinara spicy fish stew-chowder
Zuppa di pesce fish soup
Zuppa di vongole soup with clams and white wine
Tortellini in brodo tortellini in chicken broth

Pasta - Pasta dishes

Cannelloni ai quattro formaggi four cheese cannelloni
Fettuccine al ragù meat sauce fettuccine
Fettuccine fatte in casa con panna e piselli homemade
    fettuccine with cream sauce and peas
Pasta ai frutti di mare pasta with seafood in white sauce
Pasta al burro pasta with a dressing of butter and
    Parmesan cheese
Pasta al forno (lasagna) lasagna
Pasta con le sarde pasta with sardines

Pasta con le vongole pasta in white clams sauce
Pasta 'ncaciata Sicilian macaroni with cheese and
    eggplant
Penne alla diavola penne in spicy tomato sauce
Penne alla puttanesca capers, black olives, parsley,
    garlic, pepper
Rigatoni all'amatriciana rigatoni in tomato sauce
    with bacon
Spaghetti aglio olio e peperoncino spaghetti with
    garlic, olive oil, hot pepper
Spaghetti alla carbonara spaghetti with bacon, eggs
    and Parmesan cheese
Tagliatelle al sugo di carne tagliatelle with meat sauce
Vermicelli alla Siciliana vermicelli Sicilian style

Note: Pasta can be **al dente** (cooked but still firm to the
bite) or **ben cotta** (well-cooked).

Fish - Pesce

anchovies **acciughe**
baby squid **calamaretti**
clams **vongole**
coal-fish **nasello**
cod **merluzzo**
crabs **granchi**
crayfish **gamberi**
cuttlefish **seppia**
dried salted cod **baccalà**
eel **anguilla**
mackerel **sgombro**
mussels **cozze**
octopus **polpo**
prawns **scampi**
sardines **sardine**
sea bass **spigola**
sea bream (type) **orata**
sea urchins **ricci**
shrimps **gamberetti**

sole **sogliola**
squid **calamari**
swordfish **pesce spada**

Fish can be … **Il pesce può essere...**

baked **al forno**
boiled **lesso**
fried **fritto**
grilled **alla griglia**
marinated **marinato**
poached **affogato**
smoked **affumicato**
steamed **cotto a vapore**
stewed **in umido**

Meats - Carni

roast lamb **abbacchio**
lamb **agnello**
rib steak **bistecca di maiale**
chop **braciola**
leg **cosciotto**
rib **costola**
liver **fegato**
tongue **lingua**
pork **maiale**
beef **manzo**
marrow **midollo**
bacon **pancetta affumicata**
meatballs **polpette**
seasoned beef or veal **polpetto**
ham **prosciutto**
roast beef **rosbif arrosto**
sausages **salsicce**
cutlets **cotolette**
pieces of meat grilled or roasted on a skewer **spiedini**
veal **vitello**

Note: Meat can be **al sangue** (rare), **ben cotta** (well-done) or **a puntino** (medium).

Game and poultry - Cacciagione e pollame

lark **allodola**
duck **anatra**
snipe **beccaccino**
baby goat **capretto**
wild boar **cinghiale**
rabbit **coniglio**
pheasant **fagiano**
guinea fowl **faraona**
hare **lepre**
chicken **pollo**
quail **quaglia**
venison **selvaggina**
turkey **tacchino**
thrush **tordo**

Side dishes and vegetables - Contorni e verdure

beans **fagioli**
seafood salad **insalata di mare**
mixed vegetables **insalata mista**
roasted potatoes **patate arrosto**
grilled bell peppers **peperoni**
tomatoes stuffed with rice **pomodori col riso**
grilled cheese **scamorza**
fried vegetables **verdura fritta**
stuffed zucchini **zucchine ripiene**

Cheese - Formaggio

Bel paese smooth Italian soft cheese
Caciocavallo firm, slightly sweet cheese from cow or
    sheep milk

Gorgonzola the most famous of the Italian blue-veined
    cheeses
Mozzarella moist and firm white unripened mild cheese
Parmigiano regiano Parmesan cheese
Pecorino romano o sardo Pecorino cheese from the
    Rome region or from Sardinia
Ricotta white unripened whey cheese

Fruits - Frutta

Frutti di stagione fruits of the season
Macedonia di frutta fruit salad

Desserts - Dolce

In each Italian region, you will be served special sweets,
biscuits, and desserts typical of that area. Some specialties will never lack in a menu, no matter where you are in
Italy. The following are only some of the typical national
desserts:

Gelati di creme creamy ice cream
Gelati di frutta fruit-flavored ice cream
Tiramisù tiramisu
Millefoglie thousand-layer cake
Crème caramel crème caramel

For example, if you spend your vacation in Sicily, you
can enjoy the following selection:

Dolce di castagne e riso Chestnut and rice pudding
Cassata siciliana Sicilian cheesecake with dried fruits
Cassata gelata iced "cassata"
Spuma gelata di crema iced mousse
Cannoli alla siciliana Sicilian fried stuffed pastries
Cannoli alla crema di caffé crescents with coffee cream
Frittelle di frutta Sicilian fruit fritters

Cassatine di ricotta Tarts with ricotta cheese
Sfincioni di riso Fried rice cakes
Crispelle siciliane Sicilian doughnuts
Mustazzoli di erice Sicilian almond biscuits

Culinary expressions - Espressioni culinarie

all'aglio e olio cooked in oil and garlic
al basilico with basil
alla besciamella with Béchamel sauce
in bianco without sauce, light and boiled dish
bollito boiled or stewed
al burro with butter or cooked in butter
al sugo with tomato sauce
al cartoccio baked and wrapped in foil
cotto al dente not overcooked
dorato golden brown (usually fried)
alle erbe with herbs
ai ferri grilled
al forno baked
alla griglia grilled
imbottito stuffed
lesso boiled
alla marinara with seafood sauce
al ragù with tomato and meat sauce
salsa verde with a parsley and garlic sauce
crudo raw
allo spiedo on the spit
in umido steamed

Wines and beverages - Vini e bevande

red wine **vino rosso**
white wine **vino bianco**
rosé wine **rosatello**
homemade wine **vino della casa**

Wine can be... **Il vino può essere...**
dry **secco**
sweet **dolce**
full **pieno**
light **leggero**

a bottle of beer **birra in bottiglia**
draught beer **birra alla spina**
light beer **birra bionda**
dark beer **birra scura**

7. SHOPPING

Italy is one of the world's most renowned places for personal shopping. Whether you are in the capital or in a rural area in Tuscany you will always find some lovely family-owned shop, where you can buy a refined souvenir for your best friends back home, a pair of high-quality leather shoes, or a piece of the best hand-crafted 18-karat Italian jewelry. Here are some useful words and sentences you might want to learn and use when practicing the *art* of shopping in Italy.

Where can I buy...? **Dove posso comprare.....?**
Where do they sell..../where are.... sold? **Dove vendono ....?**
May I help you? **Posso aiutarLa?**
I am just looking, thank you. **Vorrei solo dare un'occhiata, posso?**
I am looking for an evening dress. **Cerco un vestito da sera.**
Can you help me find a dress in my size? **Può aiutarmi a cercare un vestito della mia misura?**
I'd like to buy a hat for my father. **Vorrei comprare un cappello per mio padre?**
May I try this skirt on? **Posso provare questa gonna?**
Where is the fitting room? **Dov'è il camerino?**
Does this shirt come in other colors? **Avete la stessa camicia in altri colori?**
It's too big/small/long/short. **E' troppo grande/piccolo/ lungo/corto.**
I will need this in a bigger/smaller size. **Ho bisogno di una taglia più grande/piccola.**
Do you make alterations here? **Fate anche modifiche qui?**
Is there anything on sale? **C'è niente in saldo?**
May I return this? **Posso cambiarlo una volta comprato?**
Can I pay with my credit card? **Posso pagare con la carta di credito?**

Every item in the store is on sale. **Tutto nel negozio è in saldo.**

The fitting room is this way... **I camerini sono da questa parte…**

There is 50% off all man's clothes. **C'è uno sconto del 50% su tutti gli abiti da uomo.**

Our tailor will make all the necessary alterations. **La nostra sarta può fare tutte le modifiche necessarie.**

We do not accept credit cards, cash only. **Non accettiamo carte di credito, solo contante.**

We accept returned items only if you can show a receipt. **Riprendiamo indietro l'acquisto solo se potrà esibire la ricevuta.**

We do not refund the returned merchandise, but we give you a purchase voucher. **Non restituiamo il denaro, ma diamo un buono d'acquisto per il valore equivalente.**

(gift) wrap **un pacchetto regalo**
to wrap **incartare**

Shops/stores - I negozi

bakery **pane e pasta**
butcher **macelleria**
confectioner/pastry shop **pasticceria**
delicatessen shop **salumeria**
fishmonger/fish market **pescivendolo/pescheria**
greengrocer **fruttivendolo**
grocery store **alimentari**
jeweler **gioielleria**
dairy **latteria**
newsstand **giornalaio**
perfumery **profumeria**
pharmacy **farmacia**

souvenirs store **negozio di souvenirs**
stationer's **cartolibreria**
tobacconist **tabaccheria**
watchmaker **orologeria**

**Clothes, shoes, and accessories – Vestiti, scarpe
e accessori**

sweater **maglione**
skirt **gonna**
shirt **camicia**
blouse **camicetta**
T-shirt **maglietta**
pants **pantaloni**
stockings **calze/collants**
socks **pedalini**
shoes **scarpe**
shoelaces **lacci delle scarpe**
sneakers **scarpe da ginnastica**
shawl **foulard**
scarf **sciarpa**
hat **cappello**
tie **cravatta**
bow tie **papillon**
gloves **guanti**
sunglasses **occhiali da sole**
sport clothes **abbigliamento sportivo**
casual dress **abbigliamento casual**
full dress **abito da cerimonia**
single/double-breasted suit **abito a un petto/abito a
    doppio petto**
evening gown **abito da sera**
wedding dress **abito da sposa**
large sizes **misure forti**
belt **cinta**
tailor **sarto**
hem **orlo**
to make a hem **fare l'orlo**

to shorten **accorciare**
to lengthen **allungare**
leather wallet **portafoglio di pelle**
handmade silver jewelry **argento lavorato a mano**

Shoe sizes - Misura di scarpe

Italian	U.S.
34	3½
35	4
36	5/5½
37	6½
38	7/7½
39	8/8½
40	9
41	9½/10
42	10½/11

Clothes sizes - Taglie

Women

Italian	U.S.
38	10
40	12
42	14
44	16

Men

Italian	U.S.
46	36
48	38
50	40

At the supermarket - Al supermercado

aisles **i reparti**
bread **pane**
canned foods **cibi in scatola**

cheese and dairy products **formaggi/latticini**
cold cuts **affettati**
detergents **detersivi**
fruits and vegetables **frutta e verdura**
meat **carni**
pasta **pasta**

I'd like a piece of... **Vorrei un pezzo di...**
I'd like four slices of ham. **Vorrei quattro fette di prosciutto.**
I'd like one kilogram of Swiss cheese. **Vorrei un etto di formaggio svizzero.**

8. SERVICES

At the dry cleaner - In tintoria

Can you dry-clean these shirts for me, please? **Può pulirmi queste camicie, per favore?**

Be careful, this shirt is 100% silk. **Faccia molta attenzione, è una camicia di seta pura.**

Can you iron these pants by tomorrow night? **Può stirarmi questi pantaloni per domani sera?**

When are the pants going to be ready? **Quando saranno pronti i pantaloni?**

When do you need your pants to be ready? **Per quando Le servono i pantaloni?**

I need them by Saturday. **Mi servono per sabato.**

Shall I pay now or when I pick them up? **Devo pagare ora o al ritiro?**

When shall I pick up my clothes? **Quando devo venire a ritirare gli abiti?**

Shall I leave you a deposit? **Devo lasciarLe un acconto?**

Here is your receipt, sir. **Ecco la Sua ricevuta.**

At the hairdresser - Dal parrucchiere

I would like to get a haircut. **Vorrei tagliare i capelli.**

I would like my hair short. **Vorrei un taglio corto.**

I would like to have my hair blow-dried/styled. **Vorrei una messa in piega.**

I would like to dye my hair red/blond. **Vorrei tingere i capelli di rosso/biondo.**

I would like a perm. **Vorrei una permanente.**

I would like to trim my hair. **Vorrei solo una spuntata.**

Do you do manicure and pedicure here? **Fate anche il manicure e pedicure qui?**

I need a facial treatment. **Vorrei una maschera facciale.**

Do you also do body massages here? **Fate anche massaggi qui?**

9. MONEY

Where is the nearest bank, please? **Dov'è la banca
più vicina?**

When does the bank open/close? **Quando apre/chiude
la banca?**

Where can I find an ATM machine nearby? **Dove posso
trovare un Bancomat?**

I want to withdraw some money from my American
account. **Vorrei prelevare dei soldi dal mio conto
in America.**

I want to deposit some money in my American account.
**Vorrei depositare dei soldi sul mio conto in
America.**

I'd like to change $300 into Italian liras. **Vorrei
cambiare 300 dollari in lire.**

How much is the dollar today? **A quanto sta il dollaro
oggi?**

How many liras do I get for $300? **Quanto ottengo in
lire con 300 dollari?**

What is your fee on currency exchange? **Quale tassa
applicate sul cambio estero?**

Do you accept traveler's checks? **Accettate i traveler's
checks?**

Do you accept credit cards? **Accettate carte di credito?**

money **soldi**
cash **contante, liquidi**
check **assegno**
credit card **carta di credito**
fee **tassa**

10. ON THE BEACH

A familiar sight at Italian beaches is the pattìno, a small red and white wooden rowboat, usually used by the bath attendant to rescue people. It is also very popular among families with children, who rent it for short sailing trips not far from the shore.

Excuse me, I would like to rent a pattino. **Mi scusi, vorrei affittare un pattìno.**

How much is it per hour? **Quanto costa l'ora?**

Can I rent it for a whole day? **Posso affittarlo per tutta la giornata?**

Shall I pay now or later? **Pago ora o al rientro?**

How many people can fit on the pattino? **Quante persone possono usare il pattìno?**

Where can I rent a deck chair? **Dove affittano le sdraie?**

At what time shall I return the deck chair? **A che ora devo restituire la sdraia?**

Excuse me, what does that red flag mean? **Bagnino, cosa significa la bandiera rossa?**

How far am I allowed to swim here? **Quanto a largo posso nuotare?**

Where can I buy a bottle of water on the beach? **Dove posso comprare una bottiglia d'acqua sulla spiaggia?**

May our kids listen to the boom box (radio) at the beach? **I ragazzi possono ascolare la radio sulla spiaggia?**

Is this a public beach? **E' una spiaggia pubblica?**

Are there private beaches along this coast? **Ci sono spiagge private sulla costa?**

Is there a nudist beach? **C'è una spiaggia per nudisti?**

bathhouse **stabilimento balneare**
beach **spiaggia**
beach chair **sedia a sdraio (sdraia)**
beachgoers **bagnanti**

beach/sun umbrella **ombrellone**
flippers **pinne**
jellyfish **medusa**
lifeguard **bagnino**
mask and snorkel **maschera e boccale**
No bathing! (red flag) **Divieto di balneazione!**
    (bandiera rossa)
nudists **(campo) nudisti**
sand **sabbia**
sea urchin **riccio di mare**
sun block **crema solare**
sunglasses **occhiali da sole**
tanning lotion **crema abbronzante**
(beach) towel **asciugamano da mare**

11. HEALTH

doctor **dottore**
hospital **ospedale**
emergency room **pronto soccorso**

Can I see a doctor, please? **Posso vedere un dottore,
    per favore?**
Call an ambulance! **Chiamate un'ambulanza!**

I feel bad. **Sto male.**
I don't feel well. **Non mi sento bene.**
I feel sick. **Mi sento male.**
I feel terrible! **Mi sento malissimo!**

I have a headache. **Mi fa male la testa.**
I have a toothache. **Mi fa male un dente.**
My right/left ear is bothering me. **Mi fa male l'orecchio
    destro/sinistro.**
I have got an earache. **Ho mal d'orecchie.**
My eyes are itching. **Mi bruciano gli occhi.**

I have diarrhea. **Ho la diarrea.**
My belly aches. **Mi fa male la pancia.**
I am constipated. **Sono costipato.**
I have diarrhea and I vomit. **Ho diarrea e vomito.**
I vomit and I am nauseous. **Ho vomito e nausea.**
I have cramps. **Ho i crampi.**

My foot hurts. **Mi fa male un piede.**
My legs are hurting. **Mi fanno male le gambe.**
My arm hurts. **Mi fa male il braccio.**
I have a stiff neck. **Ho il torcicollo.**
I have a backache. **Ho mal di schiena.**
I think my ... is/are broken. **Credo di avere un/il ...
    rotto/i.**

I have a fever. **Ho la febbre.**
I have an allergy. **Ho un'allergia.**

I have the flu. **Ho l'influenza.**
I have a sore throat. **Ho mal di gola.**
I have a cough. **Ho la tosse.**
I have sinusitis. **Ho la sinusite.**
I've got a cold. **Ho il raffreddore.**
I've got asthma. **Ho l'asma.**
I have a pain in my chest. **Ho dolore al petto.**
I have a nosebleed. **Mi sanguina il naso.**

I have palpitations. **Ho le palpitazioni.**
I can't sleep at night. **Non dormo la notte.**
I have high blood pressure. **Ho la pressione alta.**
I have low blood pressure. **Ho la pressione bassa.**
I suffer from diabetes. **Ho il diabete.**
I suffer from rheumatism. **Ho i reumatismi.**

I have premenstrual pain. **Ho i dolori premestruali.**
I am pregnant. **Sono incinta.**
I take birth control pills. **Prendo la pillola
    anticoncezionale.**

Can you give me an anesthetic? **Può darmi un
    anestetico, per piacere?**
Doctor, what do you think it is? **Cosa crede che sia,
    Dottore?**
What caused it? **Qual'è la causa?**
It's the first time I'm feeling like this. **È la prima volta
    che mi capita.**
What does the x-ray show? **Cosa mostrano le lastre?**
Is it serious, doctor? **È grave, Dottore?**
It's nothing serious. **Non è niente di grave.**

Where is the nearest pharmacy, please? **Per favore,
    dov'è la farmacia più vicina?**
I am looking for a pharmacy. **Cerco una farmacia,
    per favore.**
What kind of medicine is this? **Che tipo di medicina è?**
I am allergic to ... **Sono allergico a ...**
Shall I swallow or chew it? **La devo ingoiare o masticare?**

Before or after meals? **Prima o dopo i pasti?**

How many times a day shall I take it? **Quante volte al giorno devo prenderla?**

Does it have side effects? **Ha effetti collaterali?**

Will it make me dizzy? **Mi darà stordimento?**

Shall I take this pill with water? **Devo prendere questa pillola con l'acqua?**

12. EMERGENCIES

Thief! **Al ladro!**

Help! **Aiuto!**

Leave me alone! **Mi lasci in pace!**

Go away! **Vada via!**

I was robbed! **Mi hanno derubato!**

Someone call the police! **Chiamate la polizia!**

I was attacked. **Mi hanno attaccato.**

They stole my purse with my passport and my wallet.
   Mi hanno portato via la borsa con dentro il passaporto e il portafoglio.

They snatched my necklace! **Mi hanno scippato la catenina!**

I need an interpreter. **Ho bisogno di un interprete.**

I need to contact the American Consulate. **Voglio parlare con il Consolato Americano.**

I am innocent! **Sono innocente!**

That's him/her (pointing out a person). **E' lui il colpevole!**

I haven't seen who did it. **Non ho visto chi è stato.**

Call an ambulance! **Chiamate un'ambulanza!**

Is there a doctor here? **C'è un dottore?**

There was an accident. **C'è stato un incidente.**

He suddenly felt sick. **Si è sentito male improvvisamente.**

He fainted. **E' svenuto.**

Hurry! **Presto!**

Fire! **Al fuoco!**

Call the firemen! **Chiamate i pompieri!**

Where is the hydrant? **Dove sono le pompe?**

To the fire escape stairs! **Tutti alle scale antincendio!**

Run! **Correte!**

There is a gas leak! **C'è una fuga di gas!**

There was a short circuit. **C'è stato un corto circuito.**

13. NUMBERS & MEASURES

Numbers - Numeri

1	uno
2	due
3	tre
4	quattro
5	cinque
6	sei
7	sette
8	otto
9	nove
10	dieci
11	undici
12	dodici
13	tredici
14	quattordici
15	quindici
16	sedici
17	diciassette
18	diciotto
19	diciannove
20	venti
21	ventuno
22	ventidue
23	ventitre
24	ventiquattro
25	venticinque
26	ventisei
27	ventisette
28	ventotto
29	ventinove
30	trenta
40	quaranta
50	cinquanta
60	sessanta
70	settanta

80	ottanta
90	novanta
100	cento
1000	mille

In Italian numbers over 1,000 are separated by a dot or a space and not by a comma.

10.000	diecimila
20.000	ventimila
30.000	trentamila
40.000	quarantamila
50.000	cinquantamila
60.000	sessantamila
70.000	settantamila
80.000	ottantamila
90.000	novantamila
100.000	centomila
200.000	duecentomila
300.000	trecentomila
400.000	quattrocentomila
500.000	cinquecentomila
600.000	seicentomila
700.000	settecentomila
800.000	ottocentomila
900.000	novecentomila
1.000.000	un milione
25.000	venticinquemila
55.500	cinquantacinquemila cinquecento
120.000	centoventimila
650.000	seicentocinquantamila
1.450.000	un milione quattrocentocinquantamila

Cardinal numbers - Numeri cardinali

1st	**primo**
2nd	**secondo**
3rd	**terzo**
4th	**quarto**
5th	**quinto**
6th	**sesto**
7th	**settimo**
8th	**ottavo**
9th	**nono**
10th	**decimo**
11th	**undicesimo**
12th	**dodicesimo**
13th	**tredicesimo**
14th	**quattordicesimo**
15th	**quindicesimo**
16th	**sedicesimo**
17th	**diciassettesimo**
18th	**diciottesimo**
19th	**diciannovesimo**
20th	**ventesimo**
21st	**ventunesimo**
22th	**ventiduesimo**
23rd	**ventitreesimo**
24th	**ventiquattresimo**
25th	**venticinquesimo**
26th	**ventiseiesimo**
27th	**ventisettesimo**
28th	**ventottesimo**
29th	**ventinovesimo**
30th	**trentesimo**

Weight - Pesi

g (grammo)
hg (etto, ettogrammo)
kg (chilo, chilogrammo)
l (litro)

100 g = 1 etto = 3.5 oz
200 g = 2 etti = 7.0 oz
500 g = mezzo kilo (½ kg) = 1.1 lbs
1 kg = 1000 g = 2.2 lbs
1 l = 1.06 U.S. quarts

Measures - Misure

m (metro)
cm (centimetro)
km (chilometro)

1 km (kilometer) = 0.62 miglia (miles)
1 m (meter) = 1.09 iarde (yards)
1 cm (centimeter) = 0.39 pollici (inches)

1 miglio (mile) = 1.61 km (kilometers)
1 iarda (yard) = 0.91 m (meters)
1 pollice (inch) = 2.54 cm (centimeters)

Temperature - Temperatura

°C	°F	
100°	212°	
38°	100°	
36,9°	98.4°	(body temperature - temperatura corporea)
0°	32°	
-20°	-4°	

14. TIME

Days of the week - Giorni della settimana

Monday **Lunedì**
Tuesday **Martedì**
Wednesday **Mercoledì**
Thursday **Giovedì**
Friday **Venerdì**
Saturday **Sabato**
Sunday **Domenica**

Months of the year - Mesi dell'anno

January **Gennaio**
February **Febbraio**
March **Marzo**
April **Aprile**
May **Maggio**
June **Giugno**
July **Luglio**
August **Agosto**
September **Settembre**
October **Ottobre**
November **Novembre**
December **Dicembre**

The four seasons - Le quattro stagioni

Spring **Primavera**
Summer **Estate**
Autumn **Autunno**
Winter **Inverno**

What time is it? - Che ore sono?

1:00 A.M./P.M. **(È) l' una**
2:00 A.M./P.M. **(Sono) le due**
3:00 A.M./P.M. **(Sono) le tre**
4:00 A.M./P.M. **(Sono) le quattro**
5:00 A.M./P.M. **(Sono) le cinque**
10:00 **(Sono) le dieci**
12:00 **(Sono) le dodici; è mezzogiorno**
12:00 A.M. **è mezzanotte**
2:10 **le due e dieci**
2:15 **le due e un quarto**
2:20 **le due e venti**
2:25 **le due e venticinque**
2:30 **le due e trenta** *or* **le due e mezza**
2:35 **le due e trentacinque**
2:40 **le due e quaranta** *or* **venti minuti alle tre**
2:45 **le due e quarantacinque** *or* **un quarto alle tre**
2:50 **le due e cinquanta** *or* **dieci minuti alle tre**
2:55 **le due e cinquantacinque** *or* **cinque minuti alle tre**

At what time...? - A che ora...?

at 2:30 **alle due e mezzo**
at 3:20 **alle tre e venti**
at 5:35 **alle cinque e trentacinque**

15. GEOGRAPHY

The regions of Italy - Le regioni d'Italia

Region (Regione)	Regional capital (Capoluogo di provincia)
Valle D'Aosta	Aosta
Piemonte	Torino (Turin)
Lombardia	Milano (Milan)
Alto Adige	Bolzano
Trentino	Trento
Friuli-Venezia-Giulia	Trieste
Veneto	Venezia (Venice)
Liguria	Genova (Genoa)
Emilia-Romagna	Bologna
Toscana (Tuscany)	Firenze (Florence)
Umbria	Perugia
Marche	Ancona
Abruzzi	L'Aquila
Lazio	Roma (Rome)
Molise	Campobasso
Campania	Napoli (Naples)
Puglia	Bari
Lucania	Potenza
Calabria	Catanzaro
Sicilia (Sicily)	Palermo
Sardegna (Sardinia)	Cagliari

Famous Italian islands

Isola d'Elba (Toscana)
Isola Del Giglio (Toscana)
Ischia (Campania)
Capri (Campania)
Isole Lipari (Sicily)
Isole Egadi (Sicily)
Isole Tremiti (Puglia)

Some geographical names - Nomi geografici

Country (Paese)	Citizen (Cittadino)	
L' Australia	Australiano	(Australia)
L'Afganistan	Afgano	(Afghanistan)
L'Albania	Albanese	(Albania)
L'Algeria	Algerino	(Algeria)
L' America	Americano	(America)
L'Argentina	Argentino	(Argentina)
L' Austria	Austriaco	(Austria)
Il Belgio	Belga	(Belgium)
La Bielorussia	Bielorusso	(Belarus)
La Bolivia	Boliviano	(Bolivia)
Il Brasile	Brasiliano	(Brazil)
La Gran Bretagna	Britannico	(Great Britain)
Il Regno Unito	Britannico	(United Kingdom)
La Bulgaria	Bulgaro	(Bulgaria)
La Cambogia	Cambogiano	(Cambodia)
Il Canada	Canadese	(Canada)
La Repubblica Ceca	Ceco	(Czech Republic)
Il Cile	Cileno	(Chile)
La Cina	Cinese	(China)
Cipro	Cipriota	(Cyprus)
La Colombia	Colombiano	(Colombia)
La Corea	Coreano	(Korea)
Cuba	Cubano	(Cuba)
La Danimarca	Danese	(Denmark)
La Repub. Domenicana	Domenicano	(Dominican Republic)
L'Ecuador	Ecuadoriano	(Ecuador)
L'Egitto	Egiziano	(Egypt)
L'Eritrea	Eritreo	(Eritrea)
L'Estonia	Estone	(Estonia)
L'Etiopia	Etiope	(Ethiopia)
Le Isole Filippine	Filippino	(Philippines)
La Finlandia	Finlandese	(Finland)
La Francia	Francese	(France)
Il Galles	Gallese	(Wales)
La Giamaica	Giamaicano	(Jamaica)

Il Giappone	Giapponese	(Japan)
La Giordania	Giordano	(Jordan)
La Grecia	Greco	(Greece)
Il Guatemala	Guatemalteco	(Guatemala)
Haiti	Haitiano	(Haiti)
L'Honduras	Honduregno	(Honduras)
L'India	Indiano	(India)
L'Indonesia	Indonesiano	(Indonesia)
L'Inghilterra	Inglese	(England)
L'Iraq	Iracheno	(Iraq)
L'Iran	Iraniano	(Iran)
L'Irlanda	Irlandese	(Ireland)
L'Islanda	Islandese	(Iceland)
Israele	Israeliano	(Israel)
L'Italia	Italiano	(Italy)
La Lettonia	Lettone	(Latvia)
Il Libano	Libanese	(Lebanon)
La Libia	Libico	(Libya)
La Lituania	Lituano	(Lithuania)
Il Lussemburgo	Lussemburghese	(Luxemburg)
Il Marocco	Marocchino	(Morocco)
(Principato) Monaco	Monegasco	(Monaco)
La Nuova Zelanda	Neozelandese	(New Zealand)
Il Nepal	Nepalese	(Nepal)
Il Nicaragua	Nicaraguense	(Nicaragua)
La Nigeria	Nigeriano	(Nigeria)
La Norvegia	Norvegese	(Norway)
L'Olanda	Olandese	(Netherlands)
Il Pakistan	Pakistano	(Pakistan)
La Polonia	Polacco	(Poland)
Il Portogallo	Portoghese	(Portugal)
La Romania	Rumeno	(Rumania)
La Russia	Russo	(Russia)
Il Salvador	Salvadoregno	(El Salvador)
La Scozia	Scozzese	(Scotland)
La Siria	Siriano	(Syria)
La Somalia	Somalo	(Somali Rep.)
La Spagna	Spagnolo	(Spain)
Il Sud Africa	Sudafricano	(South Africa)

Il Sudan	Sudanese	(Sudan)
La Svezia	Svedese	(Sweden)
La Svizzera	Svizzero	(Switzerland)
La Tailandia	Tailandese	(Thailand)
La Germania	Tedesco	(Germany)
La Tunisia	Tunisino	(Tunisia)
La Turchia	Turco	(Turkey)
L'Ucraina	Ucraino	(Ukraine)
L'Ungheria	Ungherese	(Hungary)
L'Uruguay	Uruguayano	(Uruguay)
(Città Del) Vaticano		(Vatican City)
Il Venezuela	Venezuelano	(Venezuela)
Il Vietnam	Vietnamita	(Vietnam)
Lo Yemen	Yemenita	(Yemen)

16. THE WEATHER

How is the weather? **Che tempo fa?**
Today, it is cold. **Fa freddo oggi.**
It's warm. **Fa caldo.**
It's raining. **Piove.**
It's a gorgeous day. **È una splendida giornata.**
It's not raining, but it's windy. **Non piove, ma tira vento.**
It's cloudy. **È nuvoloso.**
How many degrees is it outside? **Quanti gradi fa fuori?**
It's 29 degrees, it's warm. **Fa 29 gradi, fa caldo.**
It's 2 degrees below zero, it's cold. **Fa 2 gradi sotto lo zero, fa freddo.**
It's 15 below, it's freezing! **Siamo a 15 gradi sotto zero, si gela!**
They say it is going to be beautiful tomorrow. **Dicono che domani farà bello.**
Tomorrow there will be a thunderstorm. **Domani ci sarà un temporale.**

weather forecast **previsioni del tempo**
cloud **nuvola**
cloudy **nuvoloso**
fog **nebbia**
foggy **nebbioso**
sun **sole**
sunny **assolato**
star **stella**
starry **stellato**
rain **pioggia**
rainy **piovoso**
wind **vento**
windy **ventoso**
snow **neve**
snowy **nevoso**
new moon **luna nuova**
half-moon **mezzaluna**
full moon **luna piena**

high tide **alta marea**
low tide **bassa marea**
calm sea **mare calmo**
choppy sea **mare mosso**
very rough sea **mare grosso**
stormy sea **mare in burrasca**
open sea **mare libero**

17. PUBLIC SIGNS

ACQUA POTABILE Drinking/potable water
ACQUA NON POTABILE Do not drink
AFFITTANSI For rent
APERTO Open
ARRIVI Arrivals
ASCENSORE Elevator
ATTENTI AL CANE Beware of the dog
BAGNI PUBBLICI Toilets
BIGLIETTERIA Tickets
CASSA Cashier
CHIUSO Closed
CHIUSO PER FERIE Closed (for holiday break)
DIVIETO DI CACCIA/PESCA Hunting/fishing
    forbidden
DIVIETO DI SOSTA No parking
DOCCE Shower
DOGANA Customs
FUMATORI Smoking
GABINETTO/WC Restroom
INFORMAZIONI Information desk/office
INGRESSO LIBERO Free entrance
LAVORI IN CORSO Construction
METROPOLITANA Underground
NON FUMATORI Non smoking
NON TOCCARE Do not touch
PARTENZE Departures
PEDONI Pedestrians
PERICOLO Danger
PRENOTAZIONI Reservations
RISERVATO Reserved
SALA D'ATTESA Waiting room
SALDI Sale
SPINGERE Push
SUONARE IL CAMPANELLO Ring the bell
TIRARE Pull